Eighteenth-Century
English Politics

Eighteenth-Century English Politics

Patrons and Place-hunters

ROBERT A. SMITH
Emory University

Holt, Rinehart and Winston, Inc.
New York   Chicago   San Francisco   Atlanta
Dallas   Montreal   Toronto   London   Sydney

Copyright © 1972 by Holt, Rinehart and Winston, Inc.
All Rights Reserved
Library of Congress Catalog Card Number: 75-175169
ISBN: 0-03-079280-0
Printed in the United States of America
2 3 4 5   065   9 8 7 6 5 4 3 2 1

Preface

For forty years the interpretation of eighteenth-century politics has been one of the battlegrounds of English historiography. Ever since Sir Lewis Namier anatomized the political structure of the middle years of the century and demolished the older views that read too much of the practice and assumptions of the nineteenth century into these decades, the exact significance of the developments between the Revolution of 1688 and the Reform Bill of 1832 has been endlessly debated. Very few of the questions in dispute have been resolved. Vast quantities of new manuscript material, much of it still imperfectly assimilated into the general narrative, have also become available in recent years, increasing the difficulty of confident sweeping generalizations. Indeed the picture that is emerging is one of frequent false starts, backsliding, and uncertainty in the development of such characteristic British political institutions as the cabinet, parties, prime minister, loyal opposition, and figurehead monarchs. Even though the answers are not all in, it has seemed worth attempting a general survey of the politics of the period, drawing together the conclusions of numerous articles, monographs, biographies, and editions of political correspondence.

The first three chapters discuss the permanent features of politics, those elements that remained essentially the same throughout the century such as the social bases, the electoral and administrative structure, the interplay of economic groups and interests, and the elaborate structure of influence and patronage through which the ministers conducted the King's business. The last two chapters discuss the interaction of three new elements in politics which helped to undermine and ultimately to transform the old structure into something quite different—the growth of a loyal opposition committed to changing measures as an alternative government, the growth of political parties, and the development of influential public opinion outside the narrow political class as a new force in politics. The result, the author hopes, is a balanced picture of the background against which the politicians acted, stressing equally the elements of continuity and of gradual change and transformation in this background.

The changes, because they were created by the day-to-day operation of politics rather than by legislation, were barely noticeable from year to year or even from decade to decade, but they were great enough over a century to transform the substance of political life. Well before the formal new-modeling of the British government began with the Reform Bill of 1832, the institutional framework of government and the character of politics had changed almost beyond recognition from what they had been at the beginning of the eighteenth century. The social classes, even individual families, in command of the system were still the same, as were most of the forms and much of the language, but all else was altered.

The king, once the very center of politics, had become virtually a figurehead, doing little more than ratifying his ministers' decisions even though all government business was still conducted in his name. The ministers, originally the king's personal choices, now looked to Parliament rather than to their titular master for the source of their power, and had acquired independent control of most of the powers of the crown. By the early nineteenth century these men were usually close political allies, and in the cabinet and elsewhere acknowledged the overriding authority of one of their number as avowed prime minister; the old ideal of independent ministers directly responsible to the king for their departments alone had been abandoned along with the Privy Council as the principal executive organ under the king. Most men in politics, back-benchers as well as active politicians, now thought of themselves as directly connected with the Ministry or the Opposition; the independent country gentlemen were disappearing along with the family clan and the personal connection as primary political groups. Organized political parties increasingly claimed men's principal loyalty as they became more respectable and generally accepted as essential political institutions inside and outside Parliament. Persistent criticism of the ministry by an organized opposition was recognized as a permanent and desirable feature of politics, and this opposition was normally thought of as an alternative ministry, not as a disloyal faction. The substance of politics was increasingly legislation to cope with new and unprecedented social and economic problems rather than routine administration and the conduct of foreign affairs, and in these matters all the politicians were far more responsive to opinion outside Parliament and the landed classes than they had formerly been. The British governing classes were rapidly adapting themselves to the problems of a new age.

My debt to the many scholars, English and American, who have worked in the eighteenth century will be evident from the text and the bibliographical essay: I have drawn something—an interpretation, an illustration—from most of the works mentioned in the latter. An occasional example or quotation is borrowed from unpublished material in the Wentworth Woodhouse MSS; I wish to thank Earl Fitzwilliam and the Trustees of the Fitzwilliam Settled Estates for permission to use these papers. Among the many friends with whom I have often and profitably discussed eighteenth-century politics, I would like to mention particularly Professors Donald J. Olsen and Eugene C. Black, and all of my former colleagues on the Burke and Walpole editions. Mrs. Winifred Scherer typed the final version of the manuscript with great efficiency. My wife has helped at every stage from rough draft to index.

Atlanta, Ga.   R. A. S.
February 1972

Contents

CHAPTER ONE

The Political
Structure

Society and Politics

Eighteenth-century England was ruled by its landed aristocracy. Although the power of the great families had been shaken under the Tudors and early Stuarts, they began to recover their wealth and influence after the Restoration, and the Revolution Settlement of 1689 consolidated their control of the social and political life of the country. By calculating marriages with heiresses of landed and commercial fortunes, by new legal methods for preserving their growing estates through generations, by astute business management and cunning political manipulation, they extended their territorial and parliamentary influence, expanded their rent rolls, and dethroned their former rivals—the medium-sized gentry—from the eminence they had enjoyed in the countryside during the seventeenth century. Such a concentration of power, accomplished by the 1720s, established the oligarchical character of eighteenth-century politics, and assured the dominance of the approximately two hundred families who effectively ruled England.

Landed wealth and family connection, rather than the mere possession of a title, defined this ruling aristocracy. A number of minor peers, usually of ancient lineage and always of small estate, counted for little beyond their immediate neighborhoods. Except for a hereditary right to a seat in the House of Lords, they were indistinguishable from the ordinary country gentlemen. On the other hand, several dozen nonnoble families, such as the Greys of Northumberland and the Lambtons of Durham, equaled all but a few of the greatest titled families in wealth and consequently in the social-political hierarchy of the country.

By continental standards of aristocracy, most of the great families were of recent origin. The Howards, with peerages in four branches, and the Stanleys, earls of Derby, were notable exceptions. But even their continued preeminence owed much to the dissolution of the monasteries and service to the Tudors. Despite their recent elevation to aristocratic status, most of the other leading families were well established by 1689. Elizabeth's great minister, Lord Burleigh, had raised the Cecils to equality with the Russells, earls (later dukes) of Bedford, who had risen only a generation earlier by service to Henry VIII, and the Cavendishes, on their way to the earldom and dukedom of Devonshire through the marriages and enormous wealth of Bess of Hardwick. Others who attained national importance during the seventeenth and eighteenth centuries sprang from families who had been prominent in their counties for generations. The Wentworths had owned three of their Yorkshire manors since 1327; the Montagus, dukes of Montagu, earls and dukes of Manchester, and earls of Sandwich, immediate descendants of an Elizabethan judge, had become Northamptonshire gentry by land purchases after the Black Death and now claimed to have arrived in England as companions of the Conqueror; the Pelhams had dominated West Sussex since the fourteenth century; and the Grenvilles, parts of Cornwall since the early sixteenth.

Even the Pitts had been considerable landowners in Dorset for a century before old "Diamond" Pitt refurbished the family fortunes by piracy and illegal trade to India at the turn of the eighteenth century. The few families who were not long landed —the Lennoxes, dukes of Richmond; the Fitzroys, dukes of Grafton, descended from Charles II's bastards; the Bentincks, dukes of Portland; and the Keppels, earls of Albemarle, descended from William III's favorites—were of equally impeccable ancestry by eighteenth-century standards. Birth was essential to membership in the ruling oligarchy, but inherited landed wealth to accompany it was the key that opened the door to political power.

The preservation, and wherever possible the extension, of these landed estates therefore became one of the chief concerns of the aristocracy (and of the gentry too). Improved legal methods to assure the integrity of the estates from generation to generation, despite an occasional wastrel or incompetent as head of the family, were widely adopted. The so-called strict settlement by entail made the heir (almost invariably the eldest son, who inherited the overwhelming majority of his father's property by the universal practice of primogeniture) little more than the tenant-for-life of the estate. He received all the revenues from the land not specifically assigned to other members of the family by the settlement, but he could not sell or otherwise alienate permanently any of the property without an act of Parliament setting aside the terms of the settlement that his ancestors had made. Thus his heir in his turn would inherit the entire estate under similar restrictions. These settlements indeed had to be formally renegotiated within the family every generation or two. The practice of entail on eldest sons itself was of great antiquity, but from the late seventeenth century the legal limitations made on the heirs' freedom of action became increasingly strict and were much more rigorously interpreted and enforced by the courts than they had been earlier. Because the landed classes too now regarded this restrictive approach as conducive to their own best economic and social interests, and were willing to subordinate affection for individual members of the family to the advantage of the family as a whole, there was a general readiness to accept and to perpetuate these restrictions on the uses the titular owner could make of his own property.

The strict settlement and primogeniture did not mean that younger sons and daughters were cast, penniless, out of the country house; but it did mean that they were rarely endowed with landed estates or with enough wealth to maintain, without exertions of their own, the position in society to which they were born. Except in the rare cases of families in desperate financial straits, they received portions in cash charged on the rents of the settled estates. These portions were normally generous enough to enable the men to meet the minimum standards for the life of a gentleman and for the women to make marriages suitable to their rank. But beyond that, the younger sons had to make their own way in the world through one of the professions, a place in the government, marriage with an heiress, or even, in large families of moderate means, through trade. The payments of these portions to younger brothers and sisters, as well as the charges for the jointure (the provision made for widows) of a man's mother—and often his grandmother too—were also levied on the settled estates. These charges often resulted in an individual peer or gentleman being pressed for ready cash for many years because the majority of his landed income was assigned to other purposes. But the insistence that these sums be paid in cash rather than by the transfer of real property preserved the estates themselves as a unit. The mere possession of large blocks of land, however encumbered with charges, gave a man fully as much political and social prestige as did a large expendable rent roll. Only the very wealthiest families felt that they could afford to break up part of their estates for younger children, and even then the majority of the lands (including those that a man's father had inherited) were entailed by a strict settlement on the eldest son. But other estates brought in by marriage or recent purchase might be left out of the settlements and given to a second or third son, forming the core of another landed estate to be augmented by another marriage or further purchases, and in turn entailed on the eldest sons of this cadet line. The whole system of restricted inheritance and the preservation of large estates in the hands of eldest sons through long periods of time contributed mightily to the stability of the oligarchy and of the landed classes as a whole, and in turn facilitated the development of hereditary influence over large areas of a county. Permanent connections between a great family and their tenants and neighbors thus formed sometimes lasted for centuries.

The spirit of deference that permeated English society was a powerful force in creating these connections and in giving them stability and endurance. Despite inescapable social and economic tensions among the various ranks and descriptions of men, most of them unquestioningly accepted the predominance of the landed classes in society in general and in the person of the local magnate or squire as part of the natural order of things. Land and gentle blood were assumed to confer special prerogatives and obligations in politics and government—even special aptitudes for such matters—not merely by the men who possessed them. The belief that "the squire (or the lord) knows best and we should follow his lead and not meddle in such matters" pervaded the lower and nonlanded ranks of society. This spirit of subordination was fostered in some quarters by self-interested time-serving and social snobbery, and in others by the possibility of economic and legal intimidation or punishment for disobedience. But its roots went far deeper.

The Englishman's deference to the wishes of his social superiors was in part an inevitable corollary of the hierarchical conception of society (not seriously challenged until the rapid spread of equalitarian notions toward the end of the eighteenth century) and of incessant preaching of social subordination and contentment with one's lot by the churches. But these influences, operative everywhere in Europe, were reinforced by peculiar English conditions. The landed classes had always ruled the countryside and staffed the national government. Even though the Tudors had curbed the independence and power of the old aristocracy at the center and in the provinces and had revitalized and extended the authority of the government, their local agents had been the middling landowners dependent on their own prestige rather than on royal grant. The Tudors' servants in administration had also been drawn primarily from the same landed class, as were the members of the new nobility which they enriched to counterbalance the old. Subsequent economic developments and political and constitutional conflicts merely confirmed and extended the local and national standing of the traditional ruling groups, so that the ordinary Englishman had always been accustomed to their unchallenged preeminence. From time out of mind he had looked to the squire, and the squire had looked to some peer for leadership. The ordinary Englishman was also naturally conservative, principally concerned with his own immediate affairs, and he saw no reason to question things as they were. After all, his betters had done a reasonably good job of running the country and of giving England a great name in the world while protecting his liberties and religion from popery and despotism. They generally let him alone as long as he tended to his own affairs and treated him decently as long as he remembered his place.

English society, although hierarchical in theory and in fact, was remarkably homogeneous and relatively mobile. No significant legal privileges or distinctions anywhere turned classes into castes or drew lines between landowners and townsmen. Instead men moved back and forth from the land to commerce and the professions and up and down the social scale as they prospered, or decayed. The landowning governing class furthermore were not absentees, known to their tenants and neighbors only through bailiffs and stewards collecting their rents. From richest peer to poorest squire they resided on their estates—managing their affairs in person, governing their localities, intervening in the affairs of neighboring towns, personally acquainted with their inferiors and sharing many of their interests and preoccupations. Because they were on the spot, and because of the unique importance of Parliament in the British scheme of things (to which one had to be elected by inferiors unless he were a peer) and other peculiarities of the English situation, the landowners were compelled to be—as most of them seem to have inclined to be in any case—benevolent and responsible rulers, free of the brutal excesses and sullen greed that so often characterized continental aristocracies. Most of them, particularly those of the parliamentary class, were good landlords, nearly as much concerned with the prosperity of their tenants and the improvement of their estates as with the growth of their rent rolls, for they sensibly realized that the two were inseparably connected. Their local standing, their political influence—even their administrative responsibilities as justices of the peace and lords lieutenant—all also depended on the freely given goodwill of their inferiors, for they had virtually no means of compelling obedience—no more than the king had the means to compel the landowners to act against their own wills. The brute or petty tyrant would find himself ostracized by his equals and ignored by inferiors not directly dependent on him. No one, from the king to the meanest tenant and crafts-man, could get very far for very long if he flouted the often tacit but clearly understood rights and privileges of those above and below him. Because the governing classes generally respected their subordinates and did what was expected of them in their superior status, they received an easy acquiescence in their domination of politics and society.

This spirit of deference to the landed classes was as ap-parent at the top of the mercantile-financial hierarchy as it was among the tenants on the great estates and among the generality of independent freeholders. Because of the emphasis on in-herited land and on birth, only a very few of the nonlanded rich, whose fortunes from trade or finance sometimes exceeded those of the great families, enjoyed anything approaching their prestige or influence during their own lifetimes. They might hope to merge with them through marriage or through the acquisition of their own landed estates. And some of them, such as the great banking family of Child and the West India mer-chant-princes Lascelles, succeeded in doing so. But even by the lax eighteenth-century interpretation of aristocratic status, such parvenu credentials could not effect full entry into the charmed circle—at least for a generation or two. The influence of the moneyed men in London—their control of the Bank of England and of the great trading and financial companies, combined with their long purses, which enabled them to buy seats in Par-liament—could have made them rivals of the landed families for control of the government, but they preferred to cooperate rather than to compete with the aristocracy. In return, the land-ed magnates treated them with respect, listened to them atten-tively on the subjects that most concerned them—government finance and commercial policy—married off sons (usually the younger ones) to their heiresses, and borrowed their money. Still, they were only on probation as allies of the ruling families.

The eighteenth century conceived of the family in gen-erous terms. It included not only the patriarch and his sons, but brothers, uncles, in-laws, the families into which the women had married, and cousins to several degrees of remoteness. Their influence, like their wealth, rested on the family estates, whose center was not the court or the London mansion that many of them possessed, but their country house. Chatsworth, Went-worth-Woodhouse, Welbeck and Woburn Abbeys, Euston Hall, Longleat and Stowe were all centers of small empires, whose lords enjoyed revenues approaching those of the king himself. They dominated their neighborhoods and whole counties through their influence over tenants and lesser neighbors. Through their position as lords lieutenant of the shires with control over the militia and with powers to recommend to the bench of justices of the peace and through patronage they virtu-ally monopolized local and national offices. Their pride and self-assurance were equal to their prestige; they considered it not only their right but emphatically their duty to govern for the king and his lesser subjects.

Intermarriage, by which the great families extended their wealth and influence, intensified in the eighteenth century, linking established families with new ones, and all with each other, so that by the 1750s most of the ruling oligarchy were united in one great cousinage: Churchills married Spencers and Godolphins; Godolphins married Pelhams; Pelhams mar-ried Finnes-Clintons; Spencers married Russells, Herberts, St. Johns, and Beauclerks; Russells married Keppels and Gowers; Keppels married Walpoles and Lennoxes; Lennoxes married Foxes and Bruces; Fitzroys married Seymour-Conways and Stanhopes; Stanhopes married Pitts; Pitts married Grenvilles; Grenvilles married Lytteltons and Wyndhams; Bentincks mar-ried Cavendishes and Thynns; Cavendishes married Boyles and

Spencers. In such a fraternity, society and politics took on the character of an extended family activity, full of quarrels and even rivalries, but based on mutual interests and an intimate knowledge of one another.

Immediately below this network of great families in the social-political hierarchy were the five to seven thousand families of the landed gentry. No very distinct line separated the more prominent of them from the lower reaches of the ruling families. They were often descended from the cadet branches of these families or intermarried with them, although the gentry were more likely to form their own subordinate meshes of blood and marriage with their social equals. They were distinguished from the ruling families mainly by their lesser wealth, but the principal source—rents from land—was the same. Their sphere of influence, never wider than a county, was usually confined to some smaller part of it; in the case of the small squire, it was restricted to his parish. Their capital was the county town rather than London. Many of them resented the growing power of the ruling oligarchy, for it had been acquired partly at their expense. They distrusted the government and all politicians and courtiers, whom the oligarchy represented in their eyes. And because this oligarchy was overwhelmingly Whig, many of the gentry remained confirmed Tories in politics; more than a few even indulged in sentimental Jacobitism—at times to the extent of joining in schemes to restore the Stuarts by foreign aid or palace revolutions—until the failure of the rising in 1746. Their grievances were social and economic as well as political because they were unable to keep up with the rising standards of ostentation demanded of a gentleman, as well as with the rising cost of cultivating political influence. Such tensions between the two principal sections of the landed class gave an edge to local and even to national politics in the reigns of William and Mary and Anne and on into the age of Walpole and the Pelhams by setting the country gentlemen even more firmly in their independent ways. But their interests as landowners and as the co-monopolists of political, social, and economic power united them more with their great neighbors than their rivalries separated them.

Although the aristocratic families upstaged the gentry,

they by no means displaced them as the masters of the country-side. Since aristocratic interests in the counties were dependent upon the lesser interests of the gentry in their own localities, the gentlemen were courted, and usually allowed a free hand in local affairs. They administered the county as justices of the peace—providing whatever local government existed outside the boroughs—and they played the major role in the commissions for the land tax, by which the landed classes assessed themselves. They had an important voice in county elections, in which the titled aristocracy intervened openly only at its peril. Many, in fact, had an independent influence in, or control of, a borough. The gentry were thus an effective part of the governing class of eighteenth-century England—in some ways subordinate to the ruling families who ultimately made the decisions, but in others independent of them.

In the towns their equivalents in political importance were the oligarchies of merchants, tradesmen, and professional men who composed the local governments and the upper social groups of the townsmen, perhaps three or four thousand families in all. The connection between the upper ranks of the professions and the landed gentry was close; most of the members were recruited from the younger sons of the gentry (as well as of the aristocracy), and those who prospered almost invariably reestablished themselves as landed squires. If they succeeded unusually well, especially in the law or the military services, they were often rewarded with a peerage. Philip Yorke, the son of an obscure solicitor of Dover, became the most successful lawyer of his time, the confidant of Sir Robert Walpole and the duke of Newcastle, for seventeen years George II's lord chancellor, and finally earl of Hardwicke. Investing part of his enormous wealth in estates in Cambridgeshire, he overwhelmed the established influences there, including that created by the Harleys, earls of Oxford (who had followed a similar path to power in the reign of Anne) and founded one of the major political families of the mid-century.

The most successful merchants and moneyed men everywhere in the kingdom were considered members of the governing class and, except in the largest towns and in London (where they were unable to control the borough corporations), so too were the ordinary thriving merchants and tradesmen. In the larger towns, such as Bristol and York, and especially in London, the eminent families mirrored the pattern of county society by establishing their own familial networks through intermarriage —a tendency that intensified in the later eighteenth century because of the increasing number of such urban families. A true bourgeoisie was forming, but in general the social, economic, and political connections between the landed classes and the town oligarchies remained close. Landed gentlemen occasionally professed contempt for trade, but a majority of them owed their estates and present status to successful commercial enterprise in an earlier generation, and they were still likely to have uncles, brothers, sons, or cousins in a countinghouse or shop. Although the aristocracy and richer gentry had ceased to apprentice their sons to trade, the lesser squires continued the practice. Even when the immediate origin of a prominent townsman was humble, he might be descended from a cadet line of a county family. Most of these successful merchants and tradesmen hoped to find their way back to the land, and by purchasing small estates and marrying into the gentry, they often did. The squire's lady was apt to be a commercial heiress, and the wife of a prosperous merchant or professional man was often the well-born but ill-dowered daughter of a county family. Squire and merchant also shared a common political outlook. The average townsman, like the ordinary country gentleman, distrusted the government, all government, believing politicians and courtiers to be corrupt by nature. Both wanted to be left alone to pursue their own affairs free from taxation, rapacious placemen, and the political maneuvering of the aristocratic connections, unless they could derive some immediate advantage from them.

The line dividing the lower reaches of the governing class from the much larger group, which contemporaries described as the "middling sort," is not easily drawn, but it had great significance for politics. It separated the active from the passive political groups, and socially it posed the stiffest barrier to be surmounted. The governing classes played a continuous role in local and national politics; the middling sort had only an intermittent voice—at elections, in the government of some boroughs, and increasingly in extraparliamentary agitation. Many of them had the vote in the more open boroughs, and in the lowest levels of local government they acted as constables, churchwardens, overseers of the poor, and vestrymen. They were the men contemporaries had in mind when they talked of the "people," but they were not the "middle class" of an industrial urban society, which still lay in the future. In the countryside they comprised the yeomen and lesser freeholders, marked off at the top from the poorest squires more by their style of life and common opinion than by their economic condition. In the towns the inferior professions— solicitors, attorneys, apothecaries, most tradesmen and shopkeepers, superior craftsmen, the growing number of clerks, teachers, nonconformist ministers, and other such groups—were considered the middling sort. Many of them, especially the tradesmen and attorneys, occupied more important positions in the social-political hierarchy of provincial towns than did their brothers in the larger towns, and especially in London, but even there they made up the majority of the voters. Before the reign of George III they were generally quiescent about national politics unless they believed that their interests were endangered. But their political consciousness was growing, fed by pamphlets and newspapers, and from the time of the Wilkes affair in the 1760s (see p. 130) their frequent interventions presented a mounting threat to the supremacy of the landed-financial oligarchy. As they came to resent the patronizing condescension of the governing classes, they began to align themselves with politicians who challenged this oligarchy in any way, becoming a new force in later eighteenth-century politics.

The overwhelming majority of Englishmen were completely outside politics. In the country, these "lower orders," or "laboring poor," or simply the "poor," were the tenants on the larger estates, the cottagers, the agricultural laborers, the miscellaneous petty craftsmen, and the colliers. In the towns, they were the inferior craftsmen and artisans (such as the weavers), the unskilled laborers who provided the muscle power for preindustrial economy, the hordes of servants who waited on the upper and middling ranks of society. At the bottom were the large numbers of the totally destitute. Except when they rioted, they were ignored. Their lot was sometimes pitied, but it was assumed to be inevitable and unchangeable; their duty was a passive acceptance of things as they were—a duty they usually observed. A few of them did have the vote, most notably in Westminster and Southwark, and in remote Preston every male actually present in the borough on election day might vote. But the lower orders were normally the compliant tools of other interests, essentially without a spokesman, for the reformers of the eighteenth century were thinking, not of them, but of the middling sort, when they demanded a widening of the political classes.

The Administration

Eighteenth-century politicians acted within and through an institutional framework of great antiquity, designed for purposes quite different from those to which it had gradually been adapted over the centuries. All the departments of the national government, even Parliament itself, had been created to increase royal power and the efficiency of the central government in collecting revenue, administering justice, obtaining the consent of influential subjects to taxation and important policy decisions, and enforcing law and order. After centuries of political and constitutional conflict, however, the king's government had been captured by his subjects. Parliament, still the creature of the crown under the Tudors, turned on its master in the seventeenth century, beheaded one king, governed without one at all for several years, and then dethroned another. Only gradually during the next century was an efficient working relationship between the crown and Parliament reestablished, as Parliament became the dominant partner in the government. The king had also lost the struggle to keep his administration independent of the control of his powerful subjects, and by the eighteenth century all the offices of state from the greatest to the most insignificant were in the hands of the landed classes and their allies. The monarchs after the Revolution of 1688 had to entrust government to men essentially independent of them, standing on their own bases of wealth and political power. The king could still, however, choose between contenders for office, which left him great reserves of authority and influence when he chose to use them.

Although the exact powers of the various parts of the government and their relationships with each other were ill defined in law and in the minds of contemporaries, new conventions of political practice were growing up which would eventually provide generally accepted definitions, particularly of the relations between king, ministers, and Parliament. But during much of the century these conventions were in a state of flux. Experiments and false starts were still being made, and contemporaries disagreed as to what was, or ought to be, correct procedure. As a result any description of the structure of eighteenth-century politics based on either the formal legal relationships between the parts of the government, or on the theory of a balance of powers in which most contemporaries believed, would reflect reality very dimly indeed.

No two politicians ever quite agreed on what the English constitution, which they praised so incessantly, really was. They could not agree because the constitution was steadily, if imperceptibly, changing—and changing in directions quite opposed to those that most orators professed to believe it should go. They talked in terms of balances, checks, and limitations among triads: crown, Parliament, and the judiciary; king, lords, and commons; king, aristocracy, and people. The more doctrinaire among politicians even insisted on trying to establish a complete separation of powers between the crown and Parliament, the popular ideal of the previous century which had been canonized by Locke and held up to the admiration of Europe by Montesquieu as the spirit of the English constitution. This theory of the proper structure of a government finally achieved complete expression in the American Constitution, the epitome of early eighteenth-century English political thought. But it had little effect on English institutions or customs, for while the orators were extolling the merits of a balance and separation of powers, the functions and powers of the crown and Parliament

were steadily becoming fused. Men were solving in daily practice the problem of creating a working relationship between
them, which the popular theory of the constitution would have
made impossible had it ever been consistently applied.

Until very late in the century the king was still the central
figure in politics. How far he exercised directly the authority
and influence vested in him by law and tradition, and how far he
allowed it to be exercised for him by his ministers, varied with
the individual on the throne. But there was certainly a long-
term, if erratic, trend toward the transfer of executive power
from the king to his ministers, and for the ministers to feel responsible for the exercise of this power to Parliament rather
than to the king. Although William III normally dominated his
ministers, and Anne and the first two Hanoverians frequently
intervened in the formation of general policy and the details
of administration, the personal intervention of the monarch
became steadily less important during the first sixty years of the
century. The decline of royal influence was especially rapid
after the Pelhams—Henry and his brother the duke of Newcastle—who controlled a majority in Parliament, decisively
defeated George II's attempt to form a ministry of his own
choice in 1746 by forcing him to recall them to office as the only
men who could staff an administration. (See page 126.) This
retreat of the king from politics was temporarily halted—even
partially reversed—during the first years of George III's reign,
creating a major constitutional and political controversy over
the proper relations between him and his ministers. George,
by reasserting the right of the king to play a continuously active
part in the government, was doing nothing improper, nor was
he even flouting established convention. Rather, he was chal-
lenging the drift of half a century of practice. After twenty-five
years of conflict, however, during which George's views frequently appeared to prevail, circumstances again combined to
accelerate his retirement from active politics. Well before 1832
the king, as an individual, was close to his modern function
of acting only as his ministers advised.

The legal powers of the crown, whether exercised by the
king directly or delegated to ministers, were immense. They

included the right of appointment to all of the major and most of the minor offices of the government, the upper levels of the church, and the military services; the right to summon, dissolve, or prorogue Parliament; to determine foreign policy, including decisions of war and peace; to coin money; to create peers and bestow other honors; and a vague, still imperfectly defined, prerogative to take any measure that seemed imperative for the preservation of the internal and external security of the realm. There were only a few, though vital, positive restrictions on what the crown could do. It could not tax, enact laws, or maintain an army in peacetime without parliamentary consent, suspend any existing law, or imprison any subject without cause. Most of these limitations had been absolutely achieved only in the seventeenth century, and all of them were enshrined in the Bill of Rights in 1689. These limitations gave Parliament a negative on what the crown could do in certain areas, but they provided no clear legal way of forcing it to follow a specific alternative policy.

Practical politics, however, made up for the defects of the law, limiting freedom of action by the crown far more effectively than any legal definitions could do, and ensuring that the will of Parliament—at least the will of the men who controlled it— would ultimately prevail. Although Parliament legally had to meet only once in every three years, the manner in which it exercised financial control (making the government's financial resources inadequate without annual supplies and specific appropriations), along with the tradition of annual passage of the Mutiny Act, the sole authority for military discipline, made annual sessions indispensable. Thus it became impossible to pursue for long any policies that were not acceptable to the two Houses or to maintain in power ministers whom they would not support. William III was continually frustrated in his foreign policy by parliamentary refusal to grant adequate funds. George I and George II were repeatedly thwarted in their attempts to advance Hanoverian interests through British power for the same reason, and George III had to give up the American war and his chief minister, Lord North, when Parliament turned against them. Crown and Parliament rarely attempted to dictate

The Bill of Rights presented to William and
Mary, 1689. *(New York Public Library)*

to each other, but the financial supremacy of the House of Commons imposed tacit restrictions on the freedom of the crown, within which every king and every minister had to act, or face unpleasant consequences. The crown could ultimately be forced to accept as ministers the men who controlled Parliament, and could implement only those policies the ministers could carry there.

The ministers of the crown appeared to be in an ambiguous position. The king's servants, they owed their positions solely to his appointment; yet they were responsible for all the actions of the crown and could be called to account for them by Parliament. In effect they were responsible to the two Houses as well as to the king, and they might find themselves trying to serve two contending masters at the same time. In fact, conflicts and stalemates did not often occur. Through a series of accidents and gradually developing conventions, the ministers were able not only to secure the day-to-day cooperation of the king's government and Parliament, but also to transfer effective executive power from the king in person into their own hands until, by the end of the century, they had ceased to be his servants in anything but name. The ministers became the real masters of the government. By their use of crown influence and patronage to build up and maintain a party in Parliament which was expected to support the measures of administration, they managed and controlled both king and Parliament. The politicians soon discovered that this "party," as well as the inescapable necessity of pursuing only those courses broadly acceptable to Parliament, could be used to coerce the king as well as to carry out programs he approved of. If the ministers were to do the king's business, the king found that he had to accept the ministers' advice on what his business must be, because they controlled the majority that alone could put it into effect.

The king was thus steadily losing his control over his ministers. Not only could he be compelled at times to accept individuals—even whole ministries—and policies that he did not want, but he was also often unable to keep ministers that he wanted or to get rid of those already in office. In theory, ministers held office only as long as the king wished them to do so;

as he alone appointed them, he alone dismissed them or permitted them to resign. Royal favor in fact remained a vitally important prop for a ministry, and its loss was always a serious blow, but it was no longer absolutely decisive by itself. A minister or ministry, however much favored by the king, that could not control a majority in Parliament or secure the support of an effective majority of active politicians could not carry on; the king had to accept the ministers' resignations and reconstruct the ministry. Conversely, if the ministers commanded a majority of the politicians and an effective parliamentary majority, the king could not get rid of them without their tacit consent; if he dismissed them he had to recall them to office.

No ministry in fact was ever successfully dissolved by royal whim alone. Inadequate parliamentary support, disgust at the uphill struggle occasioned by loss of royal favor, and personal piques and jealousies among the politicians were always equally important contributing factors to the downfall of a ministry. George III got rid of the elder Pitt in 1761 and of Charles James Fox and the Rockinghams in 1782 because of petulant resignations in the wake of being thwarted in some favorite design; he disposed of the Rockinghams in 1766 because they were weak in Parliament and unwilling to fight to retain office. His dismissal of the Fox-North coalition of 1783 (see pages 153–154) was superficially more of an arbitrary royal act, but in reality it was based on a careful calculation of the probable effects of the increasing unpopularity of that particular combination of politicians in undermining their parliamentary base. In effect the politicians themselves, and ultimately Parliament, were coming to have at least as much voice in the life of a ministry—its birth, its success or failure, and its death—as was the king who supposedly determined all.

Ministerial power was further enhanced by the development of the cabinet. Its growth, however, was a long, slow process, and it was not until late in the century that the cabinet approached its modern form—that is, a compact, closely unified group of the chief ministers, acting under the leadership of one of its members, and jointly responsible for all advice tendered the king (see pp. 163–175). Before the 1750s the very idea of a small cabinet dominated by a "chief" or "prime" minister was abhorrent to the majority of members of Parliament and even to many of the active politicians. The only superior executive body known to the law was the Privy Council, and although it had grown too unwieldy to be an effective body even before the Revolution, repeated demands were made for it to resume its ancient role. In theory all ministers were equals, responsible only for the affairs of the department with which they were charged, and responsible not to any of their other colleagues in office but directly to the king. They supposedly were to consult together only when ordered to do so by the king, and then, through the Privy Council, to give the advice for which he had asked—advice that he might, or might not, accept.

But practice deviated far from the forms. A "Cabinet Council" in a number of guises met regularly after 1689, although its composition and powers changed frequently. There was a growing tendency for the principal ministers to work together and to concert their measures independently of the king and to acknowledge the superiority of one of their number, usually the First Lord of the Treasury, whose control of the purse strings and command of government patronage empowered him to intervene in every part of the administration. But the whole system was very informal, depending largely on personalities and the exigencies of the moment. Most of the developments that would be accepted by the end of the century were adumbrated in the era of Sir Robert Walpole, but far from being fully established then, they were still generally condemned outside the Walpolean circle as unconstitutional innovations. The "Inner Cabinet" of the five principal ministers, where most decisions were made, was regarded as Walpole's private, secret, corrupt and evil council; Sir Robert himself was described by his enemy Bolingbroke as a "Robinarch."

> The *Robinarch,* or chief ruler, is nominally a *minister* only and creature of the prince; but in reality he is a sovereign, as despotic, arbitrary a sovereign as this part of the world affords. . . . The *Robinarch* . . . hath unjustly engrossed the whole power of a nation into his own hands . . . [and] admits no person to any considerable post of trust and power under him who is not either

a *relation*, a *creature*, or a *thorough-paced tool* whom he can lead at pleasure into any dirty work without being able to discover his designs or the consequences of them.[1]

As late as the 1770s the idea of party government as developed by the Rockingham Whigs, and which they attempted to impose when they took office in 1782—that the ministry should be composed of the members of one political group that would absolutely determine all policy—was considered unconstitutional, even revolutionary. Nevertheless, the practical demands of administration were pushing most politicians into tacit agreement with the Rockinghamite view. Experience proved repeatedly the desirability of one principal minister, whose will must prevail in the case of cabinet disagreements, and showed that such disagreements were less likely to occur when the cabinet was composed of men politically bound to one another.

Despite these developments the older notions of the independence of ministers from each other and of their responsibility for the affairs of their department alone remained strong. Consequently many administrations and cabinets lacked coherent direction, and there were few total changes of administration. If the king wanted an individual to stay on in a new ministry, he might well choose to do so—more obligated to the king or fond of his office than bound to his former colleagues. In fact, a ministry often included at least one man who was primarily the king's personal representative, rather than a connection of the other ministers, and although the other ministers might grumble, they usually tolerated him. Lord Wilmington, a favorite of George II and a rival of Walpole's, sat in the inner councils of Walpole's ministry; Lord Carteret returned to the cabinet as Lord President after being deposed as Secretary of State by the Pelhams. The practice was finally abandoned only after Lord Thurlow, George III's confidant and Lord Chancellor in four administrations, became so unbearable that the younger Pitt threatened to resign if he were not dismissed.

[1] *The Craftsmen*, No. 172, 18 Oct. 1729 (London, 1731 ed., V, 152–153), quoted in B. Bailyn, *The Ideological Origins of the American Revolution*, Cambridge, Mass., 1967, p. 50.

Despite concepts of ministerial equality and the administrative independence of departments, some ministers were superior to others by the very offices they held. The heads of certain departments, notably the Treasury and the Secretaries of State, in fact excercised a good deal of control over the others. A major division existed between these great offices of state, which carried membership in all forms of the Cabinet Council, and the much larger number of important lesser offices, which clearly did not. Between these extremes were offices in which the importance of the individual who held them rather than the offices themselves determined cabinet membership, or in which the relative importance of the office at the moment helped to decide it. The First Lord of the Treasury, the Secretaries of State, the Lord Chancellor, the Lord President of the Council, the Lord Privy Seal, and the First Lord of the Admiralty, were always members of the Cabinet Council and usually of the "Inner" and "Efficient" cabinets. Beyond these officers, membership in the cabinet and influence in its councils depended on individuals and circumstances. The Archbishop of Canterbury and the Lord Chief Justice of King's Bench, traditional members, ceased to attend except on formal occasions, and the continued presence of some of the great Household officers rested upon their importance as individuals: the second duke of Grafton and the third and fourth dukes of Devonshire were members of nearly every cabinet, not because of their court offices, but because they were three of the most powerful men in England. In the same way, an important politician in an office that was not normally of cabinet rank would probably be included—Lords Halifax and Dartmouth as Presidents of the Board of Trade, and even Henry Fox, nominally only Paymaster of the Forces, but in fact managing the House of Commons. Despite individual variations, however, cabinet rank was increasingly confined to the great offices and the great men who were fitted into them, so that office and political importance became synonymous.

Although at least a dozen posts were considered "great offices," most of the actual business of administration was conducted by three "efficient" departments: the Treasury, the office of the Secretaries of State, and the Admiralty. All the other major positions were prestigious, with few departmental duties. The three great departments were tiny empires, only loosely connected with each other, in which the head remained free to conduct his departmental affairs without the interference of his colleagues—so free, at times, that he might gravely embarrass them by actions that affected the whole administration. When Secretary of State Carteret was in Germany with George II in 1743, ostensibly arranging to protect Maria Theresa's imperial claims and her lands, he negotiated an agreement with the Emperor Charles of Bavaria without the knowledge of his colleagues in England—an agreement by which the Emperor would renounce all claims to Maria Theresa's lands in return for a British subsidy and hence tacit British recognition of his imperial claim. On learning the news Henry Pelham, First Lord of the Treasury, was not only embarrassed but aghast: he knew, as Carteret should have known, the impossibility of getting Parliament to approve a subsidy that reversed the entire foreign policy of the British government. The treaty was of course never ratified, but relations between England and Austria were permanently damaged.

Below the ministerial level, much of the administration was in a state of archaic decay. Offices were numerous; few that had ever existed had been abolished. Instead, in the successive administrative reforms during the sixteenth and seventeenth centuries, they had merely been superseded in function, but left in existence with increasing emoluments and trifling duties, so that the older departments, particularly the financial ones, consisted of both ancient sinecures and new efficient offices. The new departments, especially the office of the Secretaries of State, were extremely small; some two dozen individuals handled nearly all the business of England's foreign relations, colonial affairs, and—with the exception of strictly financial and military matters—the domestic business as well. This bureaucracy, such as it was, was almost wholly concentrated in London. Except for the inferior collectors and supervisors of various branches of the revenue, Admiralty servants in a few seaports, and a scattering of postmasters, there were no salaried representatives of the central government in the provinces.

Within the efficient departments there existed a division between the secondary administrative posts and the much larger number of inferior clerical positions, all of which were initially political appointments. Legally most of these places were held during pleasure, and in theory a change in masters at the top could mean a clean sweep below, but in fact it never happened that way. The necessity of administrative continuity made it imperative that a large number of professional administrators and clerical assistants stay on. When John Scrope, Walpole's Secretary of the Treasury, refused to testify before a parliamentary committee after his master's fall, it was impossible to dismiss him because no one else knew how to conduct routine Treasury business. Furthermore, a place, however acquired and on whatever legal tenure, was considered a species of property from which the holder should not be removed, at least not without adequate compensation. The result was that in the inferior ranks, particularly, a seniority system increasingly prevailed, and all that the minister in temporary command could do to provide for his own dependents was to give them vacancies as they occurred. The departments of state were honeycombed with political jobbery of this sort, but they were also staffed with professional administrators at critical points.

It is difficult to say to what extent the prevailing confusion of administration and parliamentary politics impaired the efficiency of the government; but it seems probable that on the whole, administration was fairly effective, and that the more notorious examples of incompetence, muddle, and corruption were overpublicized exceptions. Revenue collection and expenditure were surprisingly efficient: most of the moneys anticipated *did* reach the Exchequer and most appropriations *were* spent on their intended object. Enormous profits might be made by individuals in the transfer of balances from one place to another, but the troops and the fleet were supplied and paid, subsidies reached foreign powers, and the government regularly met its financial obligations. Diplomats abroad might complain that their dispatches went unanswered, but the essential structure of diplomacy never broke down, and rarely was it at cross-purposes with itself. Much of the inefficiency that did exist could

be traced to overlapping responsibilities—to the lack of a clear-
cut chain of authority—rather than to personal corruption. The
army, for example, was frequently confused by the ill-defined
relations between the commander-in-chief, secretary-at-war,
ordinance, secretaries of state, paymasters, and the Treasury,
all of whom were independently responsible for many of the
same aspects of military administration. Methods of audit and
account were archaic and cumbersome, the result of long centuries of growth with no comprehensive rationalization. Wooden
tallies still had to be cut for computation, as in the twelfth century, and Roman numerals were still used in compiling some of
the formal audits. Indeed a pervasive fear that administration
would become too efficient checked any desire for comprehensive change anywhere. The government of England worked, and
worked quite as well as its subjects wanted it to do.

By the eighteenth century the court and the administration
had long been formally divorced; the various branches of the
Royal Household no longer played any direct part in running
the country, although the individuals who held office in them
might well be powerful because of their own independent importance as great territorial and parliamentary magnates, or
because of friendship with the king. The court, at least into the
early years of George III's reign, remained the social and political focus of the country. Although it was no longer essential
to be "well" at court to make a figure in the country, royal favor
still gave one incalculable advantage in dealing with other
politicians. Court intrigues often played a major role in politics,
particularly before 1760, and the readiness with which opposition propaganda concerning "secret influence" and "double
cabinets" during the reign of George III was accepted at face
value reflected their notorious existence earlier in the century.
Ministers caballed against each other in the Royal Closet, and
men out of office intrigued to obtain the royal ear in order to
undercut those entrusted with power.

The principal members of any administration spent much
of their time as courtiers in order to manage the king and keep
his loyalty. Methods employed to achieve these ends varied with
the personality of the monarch. George I was most influenced

by his mistresses and his Hanoverian ministers-in-attendance, all of whom were amply rewarded for pointing the king in the directions his ministers wanted him to go. When the German-born Duchess of Kendal died, she left a tremendous fortune, accumulated through bribes, even though George II had cheated her of all his father's bequests by destroying his will. George II, on the other hand, was influenced by no one but his wife, Caroline, who had early discovered how to make him believe that her thoughts and ideas were his own. Sir Robert Walpole alone had grasped this fact, and together he and Queen Caroline could usually bring George over to Walpole's point of view. But even in this relationship, Lord Hervey, who was both popular with the queen and completely loyal to Walpole, was "planted" at court to keep Caroline in line, and to keep up Walpole's own interest in his absence. After Caroline's death, George II never completely gave his confidence to anyone; and after the crisis of 1746, when the Pelhams defeated his attempts to form a new ministry (page 126), he usually accepted his ministers' advice directly, despite occasional tantrums.

Under George III the role of the court in politics became more complicated. The court ceased to be the center of national life or the immediate scene of political intrigue. George's personal entourage was little more than a private household. He neither expected nor desired the same sort of continuous personal attendance by his ministers that his grandfather and great grandfather had enjoyed. His courtiers, after 1763, were personal friends and figureheads rather than active politicians. At the same time, the dependents of the court and the king's lesser servants were more regularly accused of acting in the royal interest and against that of the ministers than had ever been the case before. The trouble began when the Scotsman Lord Bute, George III's inept and politically inexperienced tutor whom his adoring student had made principal minister in the hope of regenerating his country, retired in April 1763, having lost his nerve in the face of constant political attacks (pages 78–79). George allowed him to remain briefly as principal royal adviser out of office. From these months stemmed the myth, carefully cultivated by other politicians, of his continuous secret influence during the next seven years. Bute, like any other influential figure, had his followers and dependents, some of whom were unpopular Scotsmen. These men shared with him and with George III the ideal of a monarch who would rule above political factions, selecting the most able men from all of them to form a truly "patriotic" administration. A good many other men in politics, in the administration, and around the new court—men who had little connection with Bute or with the old ministers who had monopolized office for so long—also believed in this ideal; it had been a standard platitude of opposition rhetoric for thirty years. Without any direct encouragement from George, they formed themselves into a "party" and boasted of themselves as the "King's Friends." In pamphlets, speeches, and private conversations, they expounded legally correct but politically outworn views of the exalted personal authority of the king in politics and in the constitutional structure. The other politicians were so divided among themselves that they were unable to form a comprehensive administration, so that the group of self-styled "King's Friends," many of them members of Parliament, became a potent force in politics during the 1760s, shifting their support from group to group to advance the "true" interests of the king.

Because the other politicians needed an excuse for their failure to establish themselves in power, and because so many of the "King's Friends" occupied positions close to George or were allowed easy access to him (despite their usually inferior official and social position), the politicians seized upon the group's existence to create the fiction that they formed a "double Cabinet," advising the king contrary to the wishes of his legally responsible ministers. To what extent the creators of this fiction believed it is uncertain. Those in the inner circle certainly used it increasingly as a polite cover for expressing their distrust of the king himself, whom they could not in all decency criticize openly in public. But outside this knot, the fiction was accepted as political fact. As a result all the political battles, whatever the ostensible subject—until the French Revolution introduced quite different divisions into English politics—were really fought over supposed attempts by the king and his personal allies to seize control of the administration and Parliament from the men of "natural weight" in the country who had long controlled both. The objective—the politicians insisted—was to establish an arbitrary government ruling through a subservient Parliament and a fictitious ministry, in which real power rested with the king and his "secret" advisers. Although this prolonged constitutional controversy rested on a largely imaginary interpretation of what George III wished to do to the structure of the government of the country, it did raise fundamental questions concerning this structure and the relations of its various parts to one another which prepared the way for major changes in the character of the British government.

Parliament

"To be out of Parliament is to be out of the world," Admiral Rodney told a friend. "You must first make a figure there, if you would make a figure, or a fortune, in your country," Lord Chesterfield advised his son. To some Englishmen membership in this exclusive club, this "very agreeable coffeehouse," as Gibbon called it, came easily.[2] All the sons of the great political families who had already achieved prominence or who attained it during the eighteenth century—Russells, Cavendishes, Pelhams, Townshends, Walpoles, Pitts—became members as soon as they came of age. The eldest sons of other important peers could also expect a seat as a birthright. Equally certain of membership were the heads of the leading county families. Some of them enjoyed an almost hereditary right to a county seat, and a considerable number of them controlled a borough from which they could return themselves. These "inevitable Parliament men" made up the nucleus of two major groups in the House of Commons—the active politicians and the independent country gentlemen—but they were only a small minority of the total membership. For the rest of the 558 members, acquiring a seat meant exerting

[2] Historical Manuscripts Commission, *Stopford-Sackville MSS*, vol. 2 (1910), 173; Philip Dormer Stanhope, fourth earl of Chesterfield, *Letters*, ed. B. Dobrée [London], 1932, IV, 1455; Edward Gibbon, *Letters*, ed. J. E. Norton, London, 1956, II, 56.

The House of Commons in the mid-
eighteenth century. *(New York Public
Library)*

effort, an effort several thousand men were only too eager to make during the century.

The largest single group of aspirants were country gentlemen of medium-sized estates, with no great interest in national politics but a strong desire for the prestige of a seat. A very few of them might hope to become knights of the shire, but most of them had to secure a borough interest or attach themselves (as loosely as possible, in order to maintain their independence) to one of the larger local interests. Once at Westminister they were perennial back-benchers, detached from the active politicians and following the dictates of their own consciences and prejudices.

Most other members of the House were immediately concerned with personal advancement, or even in a few cases, with protection from their creditors and the law. The absence of public spirit, though, can be exaggerated. Few men wanted seats in order to promote a cause or carry out a program, but a great many of them felt that membership was an obligation attached to their position in society. They believed sincerely that they were advancing England's prestige and prosperity by what they did in Parliament. For the politically ambitious a seat was essential, and if they did not have an established parliamentary interest of their own, they attached themselves to one of the aristocratic factions. Permanent government administrators had to have parliamentary seats to remain in office, and these were the most likely candidates for the few boroughs where the government maintained a dominant interest. Still other men were looking for places, pensions, or honors for themselves or some dependent, and an active participation in politics, almost always in support of the incumbent ministry, was the best way to get what they wanted.

Professional advancement in the upper reaches of the law, the army, and the navy was also hastened by membership. Every House contained a large group of lawyers and military and naval officers with just such promotions in mind. For them a general support of government was the surest road to preferment, but a temporary alliance with one of the factions in opposition might well hasten the process. As a result, a majority of the ambitious lawyers and many of the military officers in the House took a far more prominent part in politics than did most country gentlemen and professional place-hunters. Ambitious and successful lawyers were particularly likely to become active politicians and at the same time to mold their politics to their quest for advancement and profit. Three of the most lucrative and prestigious government posts were legal—Attorney-General, Solicitor-General, and Lord Chancellor—and several other legal posts in the ministry's gift were well worth a man's possession. Most of the Chief Justices of the King's Bench and Common Pleas reached their places through politics, and although parliamentary service played a less conspicuous part in the appointments of the other judges, it was a useful step toward this goal. Competition for all these places was exceptionally keen because ambitious lawyers were many and posts were few. As a result various contenders attached themselves to the competing factions, often becoming their most prominent spokesmen in debates. They were, however, unreliable in their attachments. When the office they coveted became vacant they were easily tempted away from their friends, if they happened to be in opposition; or if they formed part of the ministry, they were unwilling to resign and follow their former chiefs out of office. Sometimes professional cupidity overwhelmed a man to a disastrous degree. Charles Yorke, the son of Lord Hardwicke, the duke of Newcastle's closest associate, failed to follow the duke out of office in 1762, and even accepted a patent of legal precedence from George Grenville. After much hesitation, he finally resigned in November 1763 and was returned to office with his traditional friends in the Rockingham administration. Again unwilling to resign with them, after torments of indecision, he finally accepted the Lord Chancellorship from their rivals in 1770. The strain between loyalty to his friends and his own ambition was so great that his sudden death a few days later was generally attributed to suicide.

Less dramatic, but not dissimilar, was the career of Alexander Wedderburne, Lord Loughborough, who entered politics as a protégé of Bute, transferred his loyalty to George Grenville, and then attached himself to Frederick, Lord North. Rewarded at last with the chief justiceship of the Common Pleas and a peerage, he felt obliged to follow North into opposition in 1782. That he remained there for ten years, and acted as one of the principal opposition speakers in the House of Lords, was primarily because the remaining object of his ambition, the position of Lord Chancellor, was held by Lord Thurlow, a personal favorite of the king. When Pitt forced Thurlow to resign in 1792, he offered the position to Loughborough, who first attempted to arrange a coalition between the conservative wing of Opposition and the ministry. When this failed, he became the first member of the old opposition to accept office in the Pitt ministry.

Advancement in the army and navy was never as completely confounded with politics as was advancement in the upper reaches of the law because all the Hanoverian kings insisted on professional competence in the higher commands of the army, and no degree of political importance could turn a landlubber into the captain of a man-of-war. Nevertheless military promotion at all ranks was assisted by a seat in Parliament. An officer who regularly supported the ministry had no difficulty in purchasing commissions or in being appointed to the command of prestigious regiments or lucrative military sinecures, such as the governorships of nonexistent fortresses. Progress and success in a military career, nearly as much as in the other professions, were most rapidly achieved by shifting one's political alliances.

The numerous merchants and financiers (usually about sixty) sat in Parliament, not so much to watch over the commercial and financial policy of the government as to get or keep profitable government contracts for military supplies, the remittance of funds for forces abroad and subsidies for allies, an "in" on government loans, and favorable treatment for the great moneyed companies such as the East India and the South Sea. Any government not obviously collapsing could normally count on their support, and they shifted their allegiance with every change of ministry. The duke of Newcastle had to abandon his hopes that the moneyed interest, which he had long nursed for the Treasury, would cooperate to bring down the earl of Bute by refusing loans to the government in 1762. Like the bishops in the House of Lords and placemen whom he considered personal dependents, they demonstrated that they had been his friends only as long as he was in office. Of all the interests represented in an eighteenth-century Parliament, by far the best served was self-interest.

The House of Commons possessed tremendous power in its corporate capacity, although it did not yet claim the absolute supremacy that it later came to exercise. In fact, most of the political controversies of the century revolved around the question of to what extent Parliament, especially the Commons, ought to control the executive and to what degree it ought to be independent of it. No one any longer questioned that the Commons could ultimately call the tune by its control over finances, although its right to inquire minutely into such matters as the King's Civil List was never absolutely conceded. Even in finance, however, contemporaries seem to have understood parliamentary powers in essentially negative terms. Parliament could prevent a ministry from carrying out a policy by refusing to grant funds (and no eighteenth-century Parliament was ever overgenerous, however well-managed from above), but it rarely attempted to dictate counterpolicies, even though the several Oppositions of the century were moving in that direction. Parliament's control over the personnel of the ministry was also a negative one; it could bring down a minister, and even a whole ministry, but few were willing to claim, until late in the century, that it could dictate who their successors were to be—although in practice the politicians did their best to ensure that the royal choice would be closely circumscribed.

Parliament had become a permanent, annual part of government through a combination of tradition, laws, accidental circumstances, political convenience, and inescapable necessity. For two centuries before 1689 its part in politics had grown steadily more important. Two essential powers—control of extraordinary taxation and legislative sovereignty—assured it permanent, if sporadic, activity. From the fourteenth century its right to consent to direct taxation had been recognized, and at no time subsequently had the monarch been able to get along for more than a few years without this parliamentary boon.

Temporary expedients and fits of economy might postpone the royal appeal for money, but they only made the task of obtaining a grant of taxes more difficult when the inevitable request to Parliament had to be made. The superiority of laws enacted through Parliament to any other laws—a supremacy assumed from an early period—had been fully accepted by the 1530s, linking Parliament indissoluably with the crown in lawmaking.

By remodeling the borough charters and local government, the later Stuarts had hoped to secure the return of compliant members who would *ex post facto* legalize royal acts that contravened existing customs and laws, and who would be more amenable to royal pressure than Parliament usually was. Any such reconstruction had proved impossible, however, for the crown had already lost control of the countryside—and even of its own administration—to its wealthier subjects. Charles I had been forced, in 1641, to concede control of large areas of hereditary revenues to Parliament. The abolition of the prerogative courts and of the judicial activity of the Privy Council at the same time put an end to executive enforcement of those royal policies that had no clear basis in common or statute law, or, even if legal, were obnoxious to the political classes. All this legislation had been confirmed at the Restoration, so that Charles II and James II were more dependent on the goodwill of their subjects than their predecessors had ever been. In the absence of any significant military force, royal bureaucracy, or adequate royal income, the crown was forced to abandon local power to the propertied classes, and if a royal program was to succeed on the national level it had to conform to the wishes and prejudices of these classes. The restored monarchy had a large reservoir of loyalty to draw on, but the political history of the Restoration is the tale of the dissipation of this attachment to the crown. James II, in particular, obstinately affronted every basic prejudice of his greater subjects: their religion, their local authority and influence, their property, and their essential liberties and privileges.

The Revolution of 1688–1689, in its domestic and constitutional aspect, was the successful attempt of these influential men, acting through their institution, Parliament, to make sure that the king would never again be able to attack their religion, or change the laws and institutions of England against their wishes. They thought of themselves as having prevented, not made, a revolution. Because they intended only to reaffirm what they believed were already the fundamental laws and customs of the realm, many of the clauses in the Bill of Rights and related legislation concerning the limitations on the crown, the rights of the subject, and especially the place of Parliament in the government, were vague and imprecise. Some of the most important political problems concerning the working relationship of the king and his ministers with Parliament were ignored altogether.

The crown was indeed declared to be held, not by hereditary indefeasible right alone, but on condition that its wearer accept the Protestant religion, recognize the essential political rights of his subjects, and swear (in the Coronation Oath) to "govern . . . according to the statutes in Parliament agreed on" instead of merely promising vaguely to "confirm . . . the laws and customs" granted by previous kings. But contemporaries did not admit, even to themselves, the extent to which these stipulations changed the character of the monarchy. The crown had in fact been placed on a parliamentary basis: what Parliament had given, it could take away. It had prescribed conditions that it could enforce or change.

In the years immediately after 1688–1689 the implications of this new relationship—the ultimate dependence of the crown on Parliament—became clearer through the circumstance of twenty-five years of almost continuous war and by the end of the Protestant Stuart line. Although the Bill of Rights did not mention annual Parliaments—and it is doubtful that contemporaries intentionally planned to use Parliament's one new power, control over the army, to bring them about—the war against Louis XIV (War of the Grand Alliance, 1689–1697) made annual sessions immediately imperative. The unprecedented financial demands of war were met by a new method of parliamentary appropriation—specific grants for specific purposes—making the crown ever more dependent on the goodwill of a majority. The failure of William and Mary and of Anne to produce heirs also strengthened the parliamentary basis of the monarchy. By the Act of Settlement of 1701, Parliament, in order to protect Protestantism, passed over numerous claimants by strict hereditary descent to settle the crown on the Electress Sophia of Hanover and her Protestant descendants.

The House of Lords, because it included most of the men of "natural weight" in the country, dominated politics. The peers still played an active role in ordinary parliamentary business; except for money bills they initiated, amended, and rejected legislation freely. The government often relied on them to throw out such proposals as place bills (bills to exclude office-holders from seats in the House of Commons), which it would have been impolitic to kill in the Lower House. (See pages 113–114). An overwhelming majority of every cabinet were peers, and most Oppositions, especially those to Sir Robert Walpole and Lord North, were strongly represented in the Upper House. Indirectly, too, the Lords exercised great power over the Commons in their dual role as borough patrons and faction leaders. In the middle of the century 53 peers could either nominate or commandingly influence the return of 111 members of the Commons, usually members of their family, friends, or "men of business" in their factions, and they possessed the predominant voice in the return of at least as many more. All these circumstances enhanced the Lords as an institution as well as the importance of the peers as individuals.

The Lords were a small group during most of the eighteenth century, increasing only from 213 in 1714 to 224 in 1780. The Hanoverians were extremely averse to expanding the peerage, and new creations barely replaced extinctions through the failure of lines. There had been only one large-scale elevation (during Anne's reign in 1712 to carry the Peace of Utrecht) until the younger Pitt began extensive creations after 1784. All shades of political attitudes could be found among the Lords. There were hereditary Tories (even crypto-Jacobites sentimentally attached to the Stuarts), a sizable sprinkling of "Country party" minor peers (pages 120–121) whose attitudes were hardly distinguishable from those of the independent country gentlemen in the Commons, and of course the aristocratic leaders of the

The House of Lords in the mid-eighteenth
century. The king closing the parliamentary
session, with the Commons in attendance.
(New York Public Library)

factions in Opposition at any time. However, the majority of the peerage inclined to support any ministry because of a sense of obligation to maintain the king's government and because of their quest for places, pensions, and honors for themselves and their dependents.

Had the Lords been composed of hereditary English peers alone, any ministry could have relied on its support with a minimum of management and influence. But this task was made even easier by two nonhereditary elements: the Bench of Bishops, numbering 26, and the 16 Scottish representative peers required by the Act of Union in 1707. Both groups could usually be counted as certain government votes. The bishops had initially been selected as much for their political reliability as for their ecclesiastical preeminence; translation to a richer diocese rested on political obedience. The bishops' votes saved Sir Robert Walpole from defeat at least twice, and members of the bench were among the first of the duke of Newcastle's old clients to desert him after his fall in 1762. The Scottish peers, although formally chosen by means of an election from the whole Scottish peerage, were in fact selected by the English government acting through influential Scottish noblemen attached to English ministers; consequently, they, like the bishops, could be counted as certain government votes. Thus, while any government faced opposition—at times extremely able opposition—in the Lords, it could usually be sure of carrying its measures or of having its policies vindicated there.

The task of managing the House of Commons was not so easy. Indeed, it occupied as much of the time of the principal ministers as did their administrative duties. There were, after 1707, 558 members of the Commons: 92 represented the English and Welsh counties; 417, the English and Welsh boroughs; 45, Scotland; and 4, the two universities. The method of their selection, the inheritance of five centuries' growth, was complicated and, in the case of many boroughs, extremely irrational. The idea that members should represent the people of England in any sort of ratio to population or that they were delegates of their immediate constituents was alien to political thought until the reformers in the later part of the century popularized new democratic notions. The wishes of a member's constituents,

Burke said, "ought to have great weight with him; their opinions high respect; their business unremitted attention. . . . [But] your representative owes you, not his industry only but his judgement; and he betrays, instead of serving you, if he sacrifices it to your opinion."[3]

Every member, however selected, should represent the interests of all the commoners of England whether or not they had any voice in his, or in any, election. Furthermore, they represented broad economic and social interests. The county members were particularly the guardians of the landed interest; the merchants and the members from the larger towns were the spokesmen for commercial and trading interests. Their principal duty, when assembled in Parliament, was to balance all the particular interests of communities, groups, and individuals for the general well-being of England. "Parliament is not a *congress* of ambassadors from different and hostile interests," Burke told his constituents at Bristol, ". . . but . . . a *deliberative* assembly of *one* nation, with *one* interest, that of the whole— where not local purposes, not local prejudices, ought to guide, but the general good, resulting from the general reason of the whole. You choose a member, indeed; but when you have chosen him, he is not member of Bristol, but he is a member of *Parliament*"[4]

County seats carried the most prestige, but the members who filled them took little interest in national politics. Their chief concern was their local standing. But because the knights of the shire represented the interest and opinion of the landed gentlemen of England and because they were generally the most independent members in the House, all ministers found it necessary to court their approval. They were elected on a uniform 40-shilling freeholder franchise, a small sum in the eighteenth century, and one that was broadly interpreted to include leaseholds for life, offices, ecclesiastical benefices, and other intangible assets. County electorates varied from the 800 freeholders of Rutland to the 20,000 of Yorkshire, but these voters were not often consulted.

[3] Edmund Burke, *Works,* Boston, 1865, II, 95.
[4] *Ibid.,* II, 96.

Contested county elections were so prohibitively expensive that rival candidates rarely tested their strength at the polls; instead, a compromise was arranged beforehand among the leading gentlemen and peers of the county. Even when this failied, and the candidates appealed to the electorate, the countless local networks of influence and the open voting meant that no opinion mattered much except that of the aristocracy and of the gentry. Although the landed gentlemen resented attempts at dictation in county elections by the territorial nobility, in most counties the dominant aristocrat was so powerful that one of the two seats was apt to be accorded to his nominee—usually his eldest son, some other close relative, or a local gentleman of standing closely allied with him. When this happened, the other seat had to be left to the independent gentlemen; and in counties such as Devonshire and Somerset, where they were very numerous and there was no major peer in residence, both seats were the preserve of the upper gentry. When the county member arrived at Westminster (he was apt to be late in arriving, early in leaving, and casual in attendance), he rarely aspired to more than giving a silent vote in support of all ministers who had the king's confidence, or else he voted against all ministers on principle.

In contrast to the simplicity of the county franchise, the franchises of boroughs were chaotic. No two were quite alike. The variety of franchises extended all the way from virtual universal suffrage to those in which the vote was vested in pieces of property. Electorates ranged from the 12,000 voters of Westminster and the 7000 voters of London to the 2 inhabitants of Gatton and the total absence of residents in Old Sarum, from which Pitt was regularly returned to Parliament between 1735 and 1747.

Borough franchises fall into four general categories: the wide, so-called scot-and-lot and pot-walloper boroughs, in which all payers of local rates or all householders not receiving poor relief could vote; burage boroughs, where the vote was attached to pieces of land or to houses; corporation boroughs, where the vote was vested in the mayor and the aldermen or the common council; and, most numerous, the freemen boroughs, where all freemen by birth or admission could vote. Each of these four franchises demanded different methods of manipulation for a patron to establish a political interest.

Nomination of the burgesses for a burgage borough was the prerogative of anyone who owned more than half of the pieces of property. And although most such boroughs were in the absolute control of one man—"pocket" boroughs—occasionally even this type could give trouble to its patron. Anthony Duncombe, Lord Feversham, who owned a majority of the burgages in Downton, Wiltshire, controlled the borough without difficulty until his death in 1763. By will he left most of his burgages to a distant cousin, but he also bequeathed a few of them in trust to his daughter with instructions that they be sold for her benefit and that the cousin be given first refusal. His daughter and her husband, however, succeeded in having these provisions in Feversham's will set aside and kept her share of the burgages. Because neither party now owned an absolute majority of the burgages and because they were so incensed at each other that they refused to compromise their interests, there were violent contests between two sets of nominees, and petitions to Parliament complaining of election violations at every general election during the last quarter of the century.

Corporation boroughs too were relatively easy to influence. The governing bodies were usually small, and most of them were recruited by co-option, so that a would-be patron who once succeeded in inserting his partisans into the council could usually maintain his political influence in the borough by continuous attention to the demands of the corporation for patronage and local good works. Bath, where the 32 corporation members were fiercely independent of outside influence, was a notable exception.

The freemen boroughs were more difficult to manage; only when unlimited power for the creation of new freemen was vested in the corporation could an interest be manipulated by creating sufficient new votes to carry a favored candidate. The dukes of Bedford actually lost their virtually hereditary right to nominate one member for Bedford when the fourth duke offended the mayor and corporation by neglecting their requests and dictating their choice of a second candidate. The mayor and his friends thereupon refused the duke's request to create freemen among his supporters, and instead created 50C new freemen in one day at the request of Bedford's local rival, Sir Robert Bernard, who was closely connected with the London radicals. Bedford, by his political blundering, had lost his influence in the borough, and had given Bernard the nomination of a member of Parliament.

Hardest of all to control were the scot-and-lot and pot-walloper boroughs, which in most cases meant a large electorate of the lower classes who were much more amenable to direct bribery by any enterprising candidate with a long purse than were the "middling sort" who dominated the electorates in the freemen and corporation boroughs. The size of the electorate rather than the type of franchise, in fact, most often determined the extent to which a borough could be controlled by patrons. The great majority of those with fewer than 200–300 voters, regardless of the franchise, were under patronage and rarely went to a poll. The larger ones, the 55 towns with electorates of over 500 were normally independent, a frequent battleground for competing interests. They were nearly impossible to dominate for long, although a major aristocratic politician with great estates in the neighborhood, or a gift for subtle political management, could sometimes gain a real ascendency. The marquis of Rockingham obtained control of both seats at York, one of the largest (with some 2500 voters) and most independent boroughs in the kingdom, by backing only candidates acceptable to the town, carefully cultivating the goodwill of the ordinary freemen as well as of the local oligarchy, and acting only through powerful local interests while keeping in the background himself. A number of other boroughs—such as Nottingham, with 2000 voters, where the duke of Newcastle and several other peers had large estates in the town or its immediate vicinity—were also under strong territorial influence, but in none of them could a patron hope to dictate the choice of members.

The geographical distribution of seats was as erratic as were their franchises and the sizes of their electorates, although it was not quite as absurd as is sometimes represented, and less out of line with the distribution of population and national wealth than it became in the early nineteenth century. The boroughs were overwhelmingly concentrated in the south and were especially numerous in the southwest (Cornwall, Devonshire, and Wiltshire). In the north, where the new industrial centers were just beginning to develop, representation was largely confined to the principal county towns. Most of the larger places everywhere in the country returned two members, but so did the uninhabited fields of Old Sarum and many places that were hardly more than villages. Such "rotten boroughs" had come into existence for a variety of reasons. Some of them were decayed places of ancient importance. Old Sarum had once been a large town, and Dunwich, largely under water by the eighteenth century, had been a major port that had been engulfed by the North Sea. The Cinque Ports in Kent and Sussex and some of the West Country boroughs, too, had been important harbors, but had silted up or been bypassed through changing patterns of trade. But many of the small boroughs had always been insignificant; they had been elevated to parliamentary status by the Tudors and early Stuarts, not to pack Parliament in the royal interest, but rather in response to pleas from neighboring noblemen and gentlemen as the prestige of seats in Parliament and of influence in the choice of members grew during the sixteenth and seventeenth centuries. The creation of a parliamentary borough had always been one of the cheaper ways of rewarding faithful service.

The electoral system as a whole, archaic and corrupt as it appears in contrast to later notions of representation, in fact helped to redress some of the more glaring and potentially explosive social and political abuses of the eighteenth century. The existence of so many "pocket" and small venal boroughs provided a safety valve for nonlanded wealth and ambition. Furthermore, they served as an indirect means of increasing the representation of London, for the capital—both in population and in wealth—was the most grossly underrepresented part of the kingdom. Since a burgess no longer needed to reside in or even near the place he represented, a rich city merchant-financier who really wanted a seat could always find a boroughmonger or a willing town corporation to sell him one. The vast majority of businessmen in Parliament represented this sort of constituency. Other men, able and ambitious, but who were without an established landed interest of their own, who were without the special talents or wealth required to nurse an eighteenth-century electoral interest, or who were temporarily unpopular, could also find a seat through a patron or purchase. In fact, rotten boroughs provided England with most of its greatest statesmen. Burke began and ended his career as a member from a "pocket" borough; Charles James Fox first entered Parliament from one and later retreated to another rotten borough temporarily when the younger Pitt attempted to exclude him from Parliament by encouraging his opponents at Westminster to challenge his election there; and the elder Pitt never represented more actual constituents than the 32 corporation members of Bath. Even the great parliamentary reformer Gladstone began his public career as the nominee of the dominant aristocratic interest at Newark-on-Trent. Parliament, instead of being an exclusive preserve of the richer landed squires, contained a very wide cross section of the political classes; most men who earnestly wanted seats obtained them at some time during their lives.

CHAPTER TWO

Connections and
Interests

Next to fox-hunting, politics was the favorite sport of the English governing class. Although its members formed a closed corporation from which an overwhelming majority of Englishmen were either completely excluded or admitted only when it served the interest of their superiors, the corporation was always divided within itself. There was constant jockeying for position and power among individuals and groups. Personal rivalries ranged men against each other in the counties and at Westminster; religion still occasionally inflamed them; economic interests clashed; and questions of policy divided them. The oligarchic character of their politics intensified ordinary political activity at the same time that it prevented fundamental divisions of the sort that had occurred in the seventeenth century. Because these oligarchs were satisfied with the basic structure of their world, they could afford to differ on everything else. Only during the French Revolution, when fear of foreign invasion and domestic insurrection gripped the nation, did the governing class submerge its differences and temporarily form a united front—and even then an influential minority dissented vigorously.

The Aristocratic Connections

The fundamental units of eighteenth-century politics, basic to its whole operation, were the great aristocratic groups that had begun to form in the later seventeenth century and reached maturity in the decade following the Hanoverian succession. Bonds of unity beyond those of blood and friendship gave the larger and more permanent of these "connections" some of the characteristics of a political party. Still, the family was the nucleus of most of them, even though a blood or marriage relationship by no means guaranteed political cooperation. Territorial influence through the possession of landed estates, including if possible a borough or two, was essential. The magnate who had many relatives and broad acres in several counties was automatically a major political force.

These great aristocratic family connections had been intentionally cultivated over several generations. John Churchill, first duke of Marlborough, married his daughter to the heir of one of the most prominent contemporary politicians, Robert Spencer, earl of Sunderland; the united influence of Spencers and Churchills created by this match was then allied with that of the Russells, dukes of Bedford, in two subsequent marriages; and the three families together formed the heart of the Bedford faction of the mid-century.

The Pitt-Grenville-Lyttelton cousinage provides an even more striking example of the family in politics, illustrating the weaknesses as well as the strengths of this sort of connection. In the early eighteenth century two sisters of Richard Temple, Viscount Cobham, had married respectively Richard Grenville and Sir Thomas Lyttelton. Among the sons of the former match were Richard Grenville (later Earl Temple) and George Grenville, and the latter marriage produced Sir George Lyttelton. The Pitts were brought into the family when Sir George's sister married Thomas Pitt, a younger brother of William, a tie further strengthened when William himself married Lady Hester Grenville, the sister of Richard and George in 1754. At the beginning of their political careers in the 1730s, Lord Cobham's four most able "cubs"—the two Grenvilles, Lyttelton, and Pitt—hunted in a pack as the most vocal and able younger opponents of Sir Robert Walpole. They came into office together under the Pelhams and remained a coherent group through the 1740s and early 1750s. Then a series of spectacular family quarrels and reconciliations occasioned by jealousy, differences over American policy, and coalitions with other politicians confused English politics for the next twenty years.

The vicissitudes of this family feud prevented Pitt from forming a ministry in 1765 and added further obstacles to all attempts to unify the opposition to George III's ministries during the 1760s. A final reconciliation in 1769 set the stage for the renewal of the family connection in the later eighteenth century —that close and complicated relationship between the younger Pitt and his cousins (the sons of George Grenville) the marquis of Buckingham and William Wyndham Grenville, with several other Pitts and Grenvilles on the fringes. As a result of similar alliances, the network of relationships among the English aristocracy united the leading families into one enormous fraternity, in which politics inevitably reflected both family loyalties and family quarrels.

Admiration for a man could also provide a political bond, creating a connection even larger and more enduring than those connections depending primarily on family ties. This was particularly true of the Rockingham party as it developed in the 1760s. Only a few of Lord Rockingham's supporters were closely related to him, and although many of the principal peers in his connection were related to each other, by far the most important bond among them was their personal friendship with Rockingham. Charles James Fox became a Rockingham Whig through his admiration for Edmund Burke, not because he was the nephew of the duke of Richmond, a Rockinghamite; and William Windham and Sir Gilbert Elliot, two of the most prominent politicians of the end of the century, also joined that connection out of friendship for Burke. For Sir Gilbert, this allegiance even meant reversing his family's politics because his father had been one of the most prominent of the "King's Friends." The Chatham and Grenville factions of the 1760s too were composed almost exclusively of personal followers, not the relatives, of the elder Pitt and George Grenville; and even two of the most important members of the Bedfords, Lord Sandwich and Lord Weymouth, were attached to the group through their friendship with the duke.

Blood and friendship might unite men in politics, but they did not necessarily turn them into an effective political combination. To make them a potent force in Parliament, a third type of man was essential—the "man of business." Although a member of Parliament, he usually came from a much lower rank in society than that band of relatives and friends who provided power, prestige, and votes, but not necessarily the talent and constant application to political organization so vital to unity and success. Edmund Burke is the most outstanding example of the "man of business," but he was only the most gifted of a whole group of able eighteenth-century politicians. Richard Rigby for the Bedfords, Thomas Whateley for the Grenvilles, Isaac Barré for Shelburne, Charles Jenkinson and John Robinson for the "King's Friends" and Lord North—all performed much the same functions for their connections as Burke did for the Rockinghams. They acted as the liason men among the magnates of the "party," especially during parliamentary recesses, when they corresponded regularly with them, making rounds of visits to their country houses, keeping them informed of each other's opinions and of whatever useful information they could collect with the purpose of planning and coordinating a campaign for the coming session. They often planned the strategy for particular debates, and then played a principal part in carrying it out in the House of Commons, where most of them were able orators. They usually conducted the preliminary negotiations for coalitions with other opposition groups, or with representatives of the ministry for joining the administration. They sometimes wrote pamphlets for their groups, as Burke most notably did in his *Thoughts on the Causes of the Present Discontents* in 1770. But important as they were to their connection, none of them made vital decisions. They might suggest courses of action, but they never determined them; these judgments were made by the magnates who might, or might not, follow the advice of their men of business.

What led a talented and ambitious man to attach himself to a particular clan? For a man who lacked a useful family connection of his own, alliance with an aristocratic group promised the surest road to success. The initial choice was sometimes the result of accident, and often led to changes later. Rigby entered politics on the Walpole interest because of his friendship with young Horace Walpole and several of the younger protégés of Sir Robert. He next briefly connected himself with the Prince of Wales's interest in the late 1740s, but by the early 1750s had transferred his allegiance to the duke of Bedford, where it remained for the rest of his life. Whateley began his political career as a protégé of Bute's, but as Secretary of the Treasury under Grenville, he attached himself to his new superior, followed him out of office, and became his principal adviser. Burke's connection with Rockingham was even more fortuitous; a mutual friend recommended him to Rockingham as private secretary, though the two had never met. In all these cases the connection developed into a friendship and, for Burke at least, into fervent admiration. What had initially been the result of accident or calculated interest ripened into a personal bond.

The heart of most connections, then, consisted in a knot of peers and greater gentry, bound together by ties of blood and friendship. Outside this magic circle orbited a few detached men of talent and ambition, bound to the aristocratic core by interest, obligation, and friendship. When these three elements—relatives, friends, and men of business—worked together in harmony they were potent in Parliament, adding strength to an administration they supported or harassing it to some effect when in opposition.

Personal Rivalries and Ambitions in Politics

Independent country gentlemen regularly complained that the national politicians were motivated solely by personal ambition for power and place. They were less ready to admit that this same lust for prestige dominated their own political conduct in their neighborhoods. In fact, the gentry and nobility in each county were as divided among themselves by family and personal rivalries as they were bound together by ties of blood and friendship. These feuds, sometimes of great antiquity, found expression in a struggle for preeminence in the county, further complicating the normal struggle for dominance between the aristocratic interests and the ordinary country gentlemen.

Political activity in the West Riding of Yorkshire during the first half of the century centered around the resentment felt by the senior branch of the Wentworths (earls of Strafford) toward the Watson family, who had acquired most of the estates amassed by the Wentworths over the centuries through the marriage of Edward Watson to Lady Anne Wentworth in 1654. Their son, Thomas Watson, upon inheriting the property added Wentworth to his name and moved from Northamptonshire to settle at Wentworth Woodhouse, where his son became earl of Malton and finally marquis of Rockingham. So all-consuming was this family hostility that when Lord Strafford added an imposing new front in the French manner to Wentworth Castle, Lord Malton rebuilt Wentworth Woodhouse in the Palladian style with the longest facade of any house in England.

Politically, the two peers headed opposing factions in every local contest. The earl of Strafford, who had been one of the negotiators of the Treaty of Utrecht, was proscribed as a Tory and threatened with impeachment in 1715. He retired to his Yorkshire estates, where he became the head of the antiadministration interests, cultivating a "Country party" composed of hereditary Tory families, independent country gentlemen, and several prominent anti-Walpolean Whigs who had large estates in Yorkshire. Lord Malton, ambitious for personal advancement and political primacy in the county, therefore offered himself, and was accepted, as the principal lieutenant for the ministerial interests. He served himself extremely well, working his way from a barony to a marquessate, but he proved a poor steward for Walpole. His wealth, too ostentatiously spent on elections for a peer and a newcomer to Yorkshire, and his over-bearing manner offended the country gentlemen, including the cadet branches of his own family, and pushed them into Lord Strafford's camp. As a result, the principal ministerial candidate was defeated in 1734 to general rejoicing at Malton's discomfiture. Malton's son, on the other hand, by greater subtlety in his use of influence and the grace to follow rather than to lead the "sense of the county," reconciled the gentlemen to his leadership and rapidly won the ascendancy in the county which his father had sought in vain. But Rockingham could not pass on his power to his nephew and heir, Earl Fitzwilliam. Fitzwilliam appeared to the county gentlemen as had his grandfather, Lord Malton, earlier, to be an interloper in West Riding politics, expecting control simply because of his inheritance.

In all such local contests, the terms "Whig" and "Tory," or at least "Court" and "Country," were freely bandied about. In most cases they were primarily labels for conflicting local interests, but sometimes these rivalries, as in Yorkshire, led one of the groups into a connection with the ministry, and pushed its rival into the opposition group. In general, however, eighteenth-century politicians were remarkably adept at separating questions of local prestige from their alignments in national politics. County conflicts were so inextricably interwoven with purely local concerns that individual victories or defeats signaled very little about the state of opinion on national questions.

Roughly the same patterns prevailed in borough politics, although there the intrusion of national concerns was even fainter than in the counties. If issues existed at all, as they might in some of the larger boroughs, they were strictly local in character. Newcastle politics revolved around the preservation of the Town Moor, and those of Coventry around the licensing of ale houses and the embezzlement of charitable bequests by the governing corporation. Urban improvements, river navigations, and most frequently of all, conflicts between co-optive corporations of a borough and its freemen determined which sides men took. Not until late in the century, and then only in a very few of the largest boroughs, did national issues in the form of urban radicalism and the national divisions between government and Opposition begin to affect alignments in local politics. Rivalries in the smaller boroughs were even more personal. They centered on competing interests between two or more neighboring gentlemen, between a powerful outsider and some internal interest, between a landowner and some government department, between two quarreling members of the same family, or even occasionally between a borough patron and his own agent who had decided to take over the borough himself. Except in the pocket boroughs, conflicts could be avoided only by the constant cultivation of interests, and by compromises between competitors; even the best established interest might be destroyed by negligence or an opulent intruder.

Parochial issues and personal conflicts of interest and prestige characterized national as well as local politics. In Parliament itself the divisions between the factions and the duels between men of ministerial caliber were as likely to turn on minor points of personal concern, or on conflicting ambitions for the same office, as on any differences over issues and policy. A dispute about a new road between the London suburbs of Paddington and Islington, which the duke of Grafton favored because it would improve his property, and which the duke of Bedford opposed because it would raise dust behind Bedford House and obscure his view of Hampstead and Highgate, was inflated into a major contest within the ministry (which both dukes supported) between Newcastle and Henry Fox. Members were dragged from their sickbeds for the crucial divisions until Horace Walpole commented that the House looked like the pool of Bethesda. Projects for river improvements, canals, and turnpikes that affected or were imagined to affect the properties of important peers or exceptionally influential gentlemen or the interests of boroughs under their influence might well be the subject of as elaborate and acrimonious debate as that over foreign policy or the supplies for the coming year.

The impetus behind the conflicts between the major politicians was apt to be only personal ambition—the desire of two or more men for the same great offices for themselves and their friends. Before the reign of George III ideological differences had far less to do with politics than did jealousies of each other's abilities and of influence at court or in the House of Commons. Only gradually during the second half of the century did they begin to differ seriously about national policy. The duke of Newcastle's neurotic jealousy of members of ability in the House of Commons, including his own brother, because they threatened his monopoly of patronage, affected ministerial appointments for half a century and prevented him from putting together a stable ministry of his own. Private animosities influenced whole connections as well as the action of individuals. In an attempt to join forces in 1767 the Rockinghams and the Bedfords shelved their differences over American policy—on which they disagreed profoundly—only to find themselves unable to agree on whether General Conway, whom the Bedfords disliked, should be included in a prospective ministry. The Rockinghams and Pitt could never work together because Pitt despised most members of the Rockingham connection, and most of the Rockinghamites would not tolerate what they considered Pitt's overweening arrogance. The same personal animus prevented any real cooperation between Shelburne and Rockingham and Shelburne and Fox, seriously weakening effective opposition to the American war. This, rather than minor differences over policy, kept them divided in Parliament and intriguing against each other in London and East India politics.

Economic Interests

Although Parliament was dominated by the landed classes, the gentry and the aristocracy never conceived of their economic well-being as separate from, or opposed to, English trading and commercial interests. Landowner and merchant might disagree on the merits of a particular measure, but they all adhered to the ideal of a balance of economic interests, not the triumph of one at the expense of the other. Everyone talked of England as a trading nation, and the landowners were as eager to see trade expanded as were the merchants. Both groups subscribed to the same aggressive mercantilist foreign and trade policies, and if the gentry, who paid most of the direct bill for wars through the land tax, tired of commercial wars more quickly than did the merchants, who were often blinded by the expectation of un-limited profits to be made at the expense of France and Spain, it was not because they disapproved of the expansion of trade by force.

The underlying harmony of economic interests among the political classes rested on the diversity of economic interests represented by most individuals in politics. Aristocratic and gentry families alike had mercantile fortunes somewhere not very far up the family tree and many of them had retained mer-cantile or commercial interests of their own. The first duke of Bedford had married a granddaughter of the richest merchant and financier in England, acquiring for the Russells a major investment in the East India Company which the family main-tained. Most of the great families held shares in some of the chartered companies, the Bank, or the Funds. They were im-proving landlords, developers of mineral resources, promoters of internal improvements, and builders of urban developments —all of which linked them to mercantile interests. And for his part, the successful merchant or financier aimed to establish himself as a landed gentleman and to merge his descendants with the gentry or even the aristocracy.

The real economic conflicts in politics did not range land-owner against merchant as much as they embroiled competing segments within each group. The landed, and especially the trading, interests were not at all monolithic. Within the landed interest there were economic tensions, paralleling the social and political rivalries between the aristocrats and the ordinary gentry. Nevertheless, as landowners, the essential interests of the territorial magnates and ordinary squires were identical, and because they enjoyed a monoply of economic, social, and political power between them, this ultimate identity of interest was a powerful force for stability. The lesser freeholders, from prosperous yeoman to men who barely met the 40-shilling voting requirement, did not form a separate economic-political interest during the century. A majority of them were attached to one of the local aristocratic connections either by traditional loyalty or by economic dependence, and because they were largely apolitical in everything but local issues and conflicts, their votes belonged to the wish of the magnate. Those who remained outside these networks were likely to consider their votes as vendible commodities, available in a contest for the largest immediate reward. "The populace turn with the wind," wrote one gentleman involved in a contested county election, "being one day for one and the next for another, just as the liquor works or the terror of a potent neighbor influences them."[1] Their politics were indeed so predictable that it was usually possible to avoid a poll in county elections by a simple computation of voters known to "belong" to the various interests among the peers and gentlemen of the county.

Although all merchants agreed that England's trade should be protected and expanded, they could never agree on just how this was to be accomplished. So the many distinct mercantile and trading interests involved in national and local politics never coalesced into one uniform group that can be labeled *the* commercial interest. Instead each subordinate division pursued its own narrow conception of its immediate advantage and usually clashed with some other particular interest. The most deep-seated antagonism within the commercial interests ranged the medium-sized and smaller merchants against the great capitalists. Merchants—whatever their scale of enterprise—who dealt in specific commodities or traded to specific areas differed in what policies would most immediately promote their business from those merchants specializing in another commodity or area. A man concerned with overseas trade would not necessarily favor the same commercial and foreign policies that men engaged in domestic trade did. All overseas merchants who were not members of the chartered companies—and by the mid-century this included the vast majority of them—resented their privileges and always favored attempts to cut them down and open up the trade.

[1] William Radcliffe to Richard Witton, 1 Jan. 173[4], Wentworth-Woodhouse MSS, Sheffield, England.

In all the wars of the century the interests of men engaged in European trade were far different from those engaged in the American or Eastern trade; the latter were always anticipating gains to be made from successful attacks on French and Spanish colonies, whereas merchants carrying on trade in Europe (more numerous but less vocal) could expect their business to be disrupted if not destroyed. The opposition to Sir Robert Walpole represented their demand for war with Spain (the War of Jenkin's Ear in 1739) as the uniform desire of the merchants, but those engaged in the extensive commerce with Spain and with the Mediterranean generally, were almost to a man on the side of the government. In the years preceding the American Revolution, merchants trading with the North American colonies usually favored concessions, whereas merchants trading with the West Indies or southern Europe were likely to support rigorous measures to curb growing colonial competition in these areas.

Because the merchants' views were severely limited to their own particular and immediate interests, with no conception of their relation to the general pattern of British commerce, the politicians often discounted their opinions in the well-founded belief that men not directly involved in some particular branch of trade were better able to comprehend and balance the interests of them all than was any combination of merchants. The merchants might, at times, profoundly influence the choice of a particular commercial or foreign policy, but no group of them ever dictated overall policy. That was imposed from above, and not infrequently it directly contravened what many merchants thought they wanted at the moment.

Only one of the major divisions of the commercial interests was extensively represented in Parliament—the great capitalists, most of whom sat for rotten boroughs. Buying a seat was virtually the only way they could get in, for they were wildly unpopular in those few urban constituencies that had maintained their independence from the encroachment of the aristocracy, the gentry, and the government. In most eighteenth-century Parliaments there were about fifty members of this type; they were not the only representatives of commercial interests, but they formed an overwhelming majority of them. In the still immature

economy of eighteenth-century England, each of them represented a wide range of specific economic interests, with fingers
in many pies. They engaged in large-scale overseas trade, particularly in the great chartered companies such as the East
India and Hudson's Bay; they dominated the financial companies, such as the Bank of England, the South Sea Company,
the new insurance companies, and the growing number of private banks; they dealt in government contracts for the remittance of money and supplies for foreign subsidies and British
troops overseas, and for military supplies at home (regimental
clothing, naval goods, arms and ordnance); they provided the
government loans; they invested in mining and controlled some
areas of preindustrial manufacturing.

Sir William Baker, an M.P. from 1747 until his death in
1769, was not only one of the greatest North American merchants and land speculators, but also twice chairman of the East
India Company, and for ten years governor of the Hudson's
Bay Company. He enjoyed extremely lucrative contracts for
victualing and paying British troops in America and at times
subscribed large sums to government loans. His cospeculator in
American lands, Bruce Fisher, M.P. from 1754 to 1767 and a
wholesale clothier who defrauded the East India Company with
defective cloth, was a director of the South Sea Company and
the Sun Fire Office, as well as a government contractor for
army clothing and remittances to Gibraltar, and, like Baker, he
was a major subscriber to government loans.

To preserve and extend these diverse interests, the mer-
chant-financiers depended on the favor of the government of
the day, and most of them shifted their political alliances with
changes of administration. But at the same time, since all ministries needed their money in the form of loans and a great variety
of their financial services, the politicians had to be sensitive to
their views, and inevitably had to adjust measures in ways that
would maintain their confidence. They did not dictate policy,
but they influenced it in many ways. The divisions in 1761 between Pitt and the rest of his ministers on foreign policy and
peace negotiations turned as much on the growing difficulty of
obtaining subscriptions to government loans from the financiers

as it did on the mounting discontent of the country gentlemen at the continued high level of the land tax. The united demand of the financiers and landed interests in Parliament for peace led all but one of Pitt's colleagues in the cabinet to oppose extending the war; Pitt resigned.

The average merchants did not consider these very rich and influential men in any sense representative of their own economic interests. Rather, they thought of them as so many impediments to enterprise, blocking opportunities everywhere by their selfish, narrow financial concerns, by subservience to the court, and by blindness to the true commercial interests of the country. Such hostility to the great capitalists was almost universal among the second rank of overseas merchants in London and the outports, among men chiefly concerned with internal trade, and among tradesmen and artificers generally. It found its chief political expression in London, where politics were dominated by the struggle between the financial oligarchs and the body of merchants and tradesmen of middling rank; it is the principal reason why London was hostile to most ministries and was an extremely fertile ground for opposition politicking.

In many ways these second-ranking representatives of the commercial and trading interests shared the outlook of the independent country gentlemen: a distrust of the executive, an unthinking acceptance of the standard opposition nostrums and platitudes, a strong suspicion that all politicians and courtiers were corrupt, and a moral repugnance for the whole way of life of the ruling class. Their views had spokesmen in Parliament, for the members for London normally represented them rather than the commercial-financial oligarchy, as did some of the members returned from the largest outports, most notably for Bristol and Newcastle. Major politicians in Opposition also courted their favor by adopting their point of view because they, along with the country gentlemen and better freeholders, were what all eighteenth-century politicians meant when they appealed to, or professed to speak for, the "people."

Rarely was the ministry able to enlist the support of these merchants and tradesmen. The elder Pitt, who always remained aloof from aristocratic connections, was the only major politician whom they fairly consistently followed, especially during the Seven Years' War when he was the advocate of unlimited expansion. The Rockingham ministry in 1765–1766 also succeeded in enlisting this element behind their program for repeal of the Stamp Act, because so many of them were hurt by the collapse of the American trade, and Rockingham used them as a lever to force the king and Parliament to consent to the repeal. Likewise the commercial interests rallied in support of the new ministry of the younger Pitt in 1784, because they interpreted Fox's India Bill (page 153) as destructive of essential parts of English trade. Except for these instances, however, the merchants and tradesmen of middling rank stood apart from the politicians, courted by the various factions, especially by those in opposition, but maintaining an independent interest in politics.

These middling commercial interests, however, were so internally divided much of the time that they were rarely a powerful pressure group. Although they shared a common distrust of the government and agreed on the things they disliked, they differed radically on what they wanted. The disunion was both political and economic. As the leaders of the opposition factions dabbled more deeply in City politics after 1760, they introduced their own political rivalries into the urban resentment against the commercial-financial oligarchy tied to the government. The result was a steady struggle for control of the City between the Rockinghamites and the Chathamites, each with their own partisans in the Common Council and Court of Aldermen. A third, more radical group centering around the notorious Wilkes produced a three-way conflict among opposition sympathizers in the City, giving the government and its partisans repeated opportunities to neutralize resistance to their policies and maintain their own supporters in local power. As a result, discontent in London, which had been a powerful force in national politics between 1765 and 1770, became relatively ineffectual in the following decade, and even in the crisis of the early 1780s (see Chapter 5), unity was impossible. Radicals, moderate reformers, and conservatives were more concerned with defeating each other than they were in trying to find a common basis for pressure on the ministry.

One of the most conspicuous economic groups represented

in Parliament through the first two-thirds of the century was the West Indian interest. Merchants engaged in trading with the islands and the great planters, many of whom were absentees residing in England, formed the basis of this powerful pressure group. Because the islands produced chiefly an important raw material—sugar—and at the same time provided a ready market for English manufactures, commerce with them fitted particularly well into current mercantilist theories, ensuring the West Indian group a sympathetic hearing in Parliament for whatever policies they deemed in their best interest.

In the earlier part of the century, the West Indians, especially the merchants, were not contented with the profits to be had out of the English islands. They hoped to capture the French possessions and to monopolize trade with the Spanish colonies as well. The protection and extension of these aggressive policies, always popular, found particularly effective expression in the well-organized agitation that drove Walpole into the War of Jenkin's Ear against Spain in 1739.

Around the middle of the century the objectives of the West Indian interest began to change. Overproduction of sugar was leading to a fear of glutting the home market. Merchant and planter alike would suffer if too many sugar islands were brought into the commercial empire, and expansionist policies were quietly dropped in favor of preserving the *status quo*. This reorientation of West Indian pressure, now exerted toward protecting established trade, was instrumental in the major government decisions that helped set the stage for the loss of the American colonies. Even as early as 1733 the Molasses Act had been specifically aimed at ending the American contraband trade with the French islands, and trade regulations within the empire increasingly came to be directed at curbing the growing competition in every branch of West Indian commerce which the English West Indian merchants encountered from North American traders. The interests of these two groups diverged at many points, and because the merchants and planters were organized and well-represented in Parliament and the Americans were not, the attempts at balancing and harmonizing them made by the English government usually favored the West Indians.

The most outstanding example of the success of an economic group in the eighteenth century was the decision dictated by the West Indian interest which resulted in Britain's keeping Canada rather than the French sugar island of Guadeloupe at the end of the Seven Years' War. The West Indians wanted Guadeloupe returned to France because its sugar would knock the bottom out of the market for their own. Because their most powerful spokesman, the planter William Beckford, one of the richest men in the empire, was the close associate of the elder Pitt, their voice was heeded, despite warnings from perceptive politicians that the expulsion of the French from the North American continent would destroy American dependence upon England. Although the activities of the West Indians in protecting their interests did not make the American Revolution inevitable, they exacerbated the mounting friction everywhere.

Economic decay in the islands and shifts in the patterns of English trade lessened the influence of the West Indians in the latter part of the century. At the same time their earlier parliamentary spokesmen were merging more completely into English society. The merchants who succeeded in the first half of the century were turning their profits into landed estates; the Lascelles, for example, were well on their way to membership in the ruling oligarchy, with great estates in the West Riding and a peerage; the Pinneys, and others like them, were settling down as landed gentry. The great planters too were either merging with the landed classes and shedding their West Indian interests or squandering their fortunes and sinking out of sight. The active West Indians of the end of the century were minor figures compared to their predecessors of the early and middle years, not much heeded, even in the matter of the slave trade and slavery, on which so much of their remaining well-being depended.

As the West Indian interest was declining, a second major pressure group, the East Indian interest was rising to ever greater prominence. The East India Company, its officers, and its monopoly of the Eastern trade had affected politics in the reigns of William and Anne, because of the rivalries of the Old and New Companies backed respectively by the Whig and Tory ministers. But these issues had disappeared at the formation of the United Company in 1709. For the next fifty years, the affairs of the Company rarely aroused political controversy, although it continued to perform its functions in national life: a great moneyed company deeply involved in government finance; a major commercial interest in the general pattern of English trade; and a source of fortunes, at home and in India, which enabled the makers to buy their way into Parliament and the political classes. Their purchase of seats in the Commons was already becoming a source of concern and resentment to established families, even before financial confusion in the affairs of the company requiring government intervention and its changed position in India from a trading company to a territorial power brought it to the center of English politics in the 1760s.

The "nabobs," Englishmen who had made fortunes in India and returned to England to buy estates and seats in Parliament, were more keenly resented than any other men who followed the standard course of rising through successful enterprise into the landed classes. Their number, unity, and supposed malevolent objectives were consistently exaggerated until these nabobs posed a greater threat to existing arrangements in the imagination of contemporaries than they did in fact. The political classes in England disliked and feared them for many reasons. Fantastic notions of their wealth, created by the great riches acquired by a few men such as Lord Clive, with his diamonds and jaghir of £25,000 a year, raised the spectre that they would monopolize all the venal boroughs by outbidding every other candidate, and that by driving up the cost of seats and contested elections, they would make it impossible for the ordinary independent country gentlemen to enter Parliament without assistance from the government. They would contribute to increasing government influence because they would support every ministry out of their need for protection, and because their wealth would render other members more dependent upon Administration. Their wealth was also viewed, this time correctly, as having been obtained through blatant corruption and by the oppression of the Indians, and hence was considered more tainted than money acquired in other forms of trade. They were also believed to have imbibed Eastern notions of despotism and arbitrary power along with their ill-gotten wealth, which would lead them to support an increasing royal prerogative, thus helping to destroy the balance of the constitution and the liberties of Parliament and of Englishmen.

The reality was far less sinister. Most returned nabobs were only too conscious of the disapproval, even hatred, which their presence excited, so rather than exerting themselves against established interests, they were usually eager to conform to existing patterns and to merge as far as possible with the propertied classes. They usually *did* support the government, but normally they hesitated to take an active part in parliamentary politics, except where their Indian interests were directly concerned. And in these Indian questions they were anything but united; the Company's servants were riven by factions and disputes in India itself, which were transferred to England. Burke's vendetta against Warren Hastings owed much to the machinations of Philip Francis, Hasting's inveterate enemy in the Bengal Council. The Company at home was harassed by factions struggling for control, which propelled the directors who sat in Parliament to opposing sides in politics, and opened the Company itself to intervention by politicians seeking to obtain control of it for those directors connected with their faction. As the affairs of the East India Company became more and more of a political issue, the East Indians in Parliament became less and less effective as a coherent economic interest group.

Until the 1780s there was nothing that could be accurately described as a manufacturing interest distinct from the older commercial interests. Their leading representatives were directly involved in the production of domestic products, natural and manufactured, which they exported or sold in the domestic market; and as far as foreign trade was concerned, the re-export of foreign goods and the carrying trade were considered as important as the export of British products. Even the steady decay of internal regulation of manufacturing, and the beginnings of the dismantling of the protectionist system of foreign trade, which were to be so advantageous in the development of

English manufacturing, were conceived as being primarily in the interests of trade rather than of domestic production. As far as the manufacturing interest did intervene in national politics, it favored regulation and restriction of trade. In 1700 the import of calicos was prohibited to protect the established wool and silk manufactures, and repeated attempts were made to prevent, or at least to circumscribe severely, the new manufacture of cotton cloth within England itself. The importation of woven silk was prohibited in an attempt to nourish the silk industry. In fact, English producers were anxious to suppress all manufacturing, both in North America and in Ireland. They opposed the granting of commercial concessions to Ireland in 1778–1779 and again in 1786. Fearful of French incursions into the domestic market, they opposed the reciprocal trade treaty with France in 1786. Although they did not achieve a total victory, they won substantial modifications in the terms of the treaty in the best organized expression of manufacturing opinion yet shown through their newly organized General Chamber of Manufacturers. But these mild political exertions were nothing more than a portent of things to come.

Religion in Politics

The question of religion disappeared from the surface of national politics between the Hanoverian succession and the French Revolution, but it always lurked in the immediate background. An upsurge of prejudice such as the anti-Catholic Gordon Riots of 1780 expressed was always a danger. (See pages 118, 146.) Passions that had animated and disturbed the politics of the reigns of William and Anne were sleeping, not dead, and most politicians feared to awaken them by altering any of the laws regarding the monopoly of the Established Church, by extending the bare toleration legally accorded Protestant Dissenters, or by modifying the total legal repression of Catholicism. The laws, however, were rarely enforced, so that a practical toleration existed except in times of national crisis.

Nothing that may be accurately described as a Roman Catholic interest existed in politics. The Roman Catholics were a tiny minority composed of a few aristocratic and landed families with their dependents and tenants and, at the other end of the social scale, a larger but politically insignificant number of Irish immigrant laborers. The landed families passively accepted their complete exclusion from politics and lived in retirement on their estates, scrupulously avoiding any entanglements with Jacobitism or with the quarrels of their social equals. The Irish were of course completely outside the political classes, but their religion did serve as a focus for resentment by the Protestant poor, particularly in London, eliciting a latent and sometimes an overt antipopery in the London mob. Catholicism was still a bugbear throughout the century, and fear of its revival is part of the background against which the politicians acted.

The Protestant Dissenters were a far more numerous and politically influential interest than the Catholics, and a subject of greater immediate concern to the politicians. They had the parliamentary franchise if they were otherwise entitled to it by being 40-shilling freeholders in the counties or by meeting the requirements of any borough where they lived. In practice this meant that they were a sizable minority of the electorate in most larger boroughs and in a number of the counties with a strong tradition of dissent. Violations of the letter of the Test and Corporation Acts, which prohibited Dissenters from holding office, were so universal and so tacitly encouraged by the annual indemnity acts after 1727, that Dissenters actually controlled some borough corporations (including such large ones as Nottingham) as their most ambitious, enterprising, and prosperous local inhabitants. In many others, where the corporation was in the hands of the Anglicans, they formed the core of the anti-corporation "party" which existed in most boroughs, and could be powerful allies in attempts to upset established electoral interests working through the corporation. As Burke said of them, they were "a set of men powerful enough in many things, but most of all in elections."[2] Moreover, they formed an important part of the commercial and mercantile interests everywhere

[2] Edmund Burke, *Correspondence,* ed. T. W. Copeland *et al.,* Cambridge, 1958–1971, VI, 15.

in England. The extent of dissent among the middling and lesser merchants and tradesmen, craftsmen, and artificers may well have been exaggerated in attempts to establish a connection between Protestantism and capitalism, but there is no question that dissent was widespread in these groups, and that only the most prosperous and ambitious of them felt any need to conform to the Established Church. The dissenting interest was always strong throughout the eighteenth century, and the very fact that its members were legally unequal to other Englishmen contributed to its coherence and importance.

The governing classes regarded the Dissenters with mixed feelings. On the one hand, they were considered brothers in the resistance to Catholicism and arbitrary government, unquestioned supporters of the Protestant succession, which was still a living issue until the utter failure of the Jacobite rising of 1745. On the other hand (and this sentiment was stronger in the country gentlemen than among the oligarchy), they were still suspected of republicanism, still tarred by memories of the Civil Wars and Cromwell. Because of these feelings, ministers never seriously considered repeal of the Test and Corporation Acts, or any change in the religious structure of the country—they could not risk loosing the storms that had disturbed England before 1715—and most Dissenters themselves had no desire that they should do so. As long as they were left alone to pursue their specific interests, given greater latitude in practice than in law, and treated like any other interest group in a borough (that is, rewarded with minor patronage), they accepted things as they were. As long as the Dissenters accepted their inferior legal status, the political establishment regarded them with sympathy; some were even willing to consider modifying the laws affecting their legal position. But as the Dissenters' outstanding leaders became increasingly identified with political reform in the 1770s and 1780s, and talked of their *right* to equality instead of humbly petitioning for it as the reward for good behavior, hostility revived. The French Revolution, of which the chief Dissenting spokesmen were fervent admirers, convinced the establishment that their earlier fears were well placed, and the Dissenters remained second-class citizens until the Test and Corporation Acts were finally repealed in 1828.

The Methodist revival, important as it was in the religious and social history of the century, had no significant political impact until the time of the French Revolution. Then its direct influence was largely conservative, even though contemporaries usually lumped the Methodists with other Dissenters as probable revolutionaries. But Wesley and his followers had always preached acceptance of one's lot in this world, and the emotionalism of the movement had channeled much energy into religious enthusiasm that might otherwise have gone into political and social discontent. The early Methodists, in any case, were, with insignificant exceptions, men and women outside the political classes, and as far as the spirit of the revival began to affect some members of the upper-middle and landed classes in the last quarter of the century, it affected their political conduct only on a few unimportant issues.

Divisions within Anglicanism itself, which had been so important before 1715, were increasingly insignificant after the Hanoverian succession. The suppression of the annual Convocation of the Clergy in 1717 removed from the national spotlight the vitriolic quarrels between the normally "Tory" High Church lower clergy and the "Whig" Latitudinarian upper clergy, and although the former continued to fulminate against bishops and Whigs in their rectories and at Oxford, they became far less influential in ecclesiastical politics than they had been in the reign of Queen Anne. The High Anglican laity as a whole had been discredited and defeated as Tories at the accession of George I, and the Nonjurors, who had been so strong a prod to the conscience of all Anglicans by their refusal to violate the oaths they had taken to the Stuarts, were dying out by the 1720s. The upper levels of the Hanoverian church, the only ones with a real voice in politics, were tied to the political establishment, and except on a few minor points regarding strictly ecclesiastical affairs, ceased to be an independent voice in politics. When they intervened otherwise, it was always from secular rather than religious motives. None of the factions in national politics had a particularly religious coloring, and individuals within them voted according to their inclination on church matters.

CHAPTER THREE

Doing the King's Business

Forming a Ministry

All ambitious politicians awaited an invitation from the king to fill the great offices of state and to conduct his business for him. If, once in place, they were to succeed in creating a stable, long-lived ministry, three conditions were essential: continued royal confidence, control of Parliament (especially of the House of Commons), and the widest possible coalition of politicians and their followers within the ministry itself. Consequently the principal ministers spent as much time in maintaining and improving these bases of support as they did on the formation of policy or the administration of their own particular departments.

The king's invitation to a politician or political group was the first prerequisite in the creation of a ministry. In theory the king was free to choose whatever advisers he wished and none of the politicians, at least before the Rockingham Whigs propounded a different conception in the 1770s (pages 134–135), would have thought of explicitly questioning this right; but the royal choice in fact was increasingly restricted after 1688. Even William III was forced to give up ministers he preferred when they could neither control Parliament nor obtain the support of enough important politicians to form a stable, harmonious administration. Every king had to learn this lesson for himself: at times he had to acquiesce in accepting ministers he did not want and policies he found personally distasteful. No king could any longer make a mere personal favorite, however able, the head of an effective administration or maintain a minister in office after he had lost the confidence of Parliament or the politicians. George II was ignominiously defeated when he tried to replace the Pelhams, who controlled Parliament, with Carteret and Bath; the Pelhams then promptly forced him to give an office to the elder Pitt, whom he loathed. George III had to give up Bute, whose sole support was the royal confidence, and later Lord North when he lost the confidence of Parliament.

Nevertheless, the king suffered a real defeat only occasionally. All the Hanoverians, even George III, wanted stable administrations that would do their business efficiently with a minimum of trouble to themselves, so they were usually wise enough to choose and to support as ministers men already strong in Parliament. Such politicians could then use to the maximum advantage the strength that royal confidence conferred. Royal confidence meant so much because most men thought the king should be, as he still was, the real head of the government, not a mere symbol, and therefore that he should, within broad limits, have the servants he preferred. So the royal invitation to office carried with it the assurance of a broad general support in Parliament for the early months of a ministry, because most members believed it their duty to give the men the king had tapped a fair chance to prove themselves. Even more important, the king's confidence supplied the means (through places and patronage) by which the allegiance of several political groups could be secured for the ministry and the instruments to maintain and extend a majority in Parliament.

Controlling the House of Commons was much harder than managing the House of Lords. The Lords, thanks to the Bench of Bishops, the representative Scots peers, and the propensity of most English peers to support whatever they believed the king and his government wanted, usually made that House fairly reliable; only the ministry of Robert Harley, Earl of Oxford, and Henry St. John, Viscount Bolingbroke, after 1710 and Sir Robert Walpole at times during the 1730s faced hostile majorities there. But very few ministries were completely secure in the Commons for more than a session or two; it required unremitting attention to keep a working majority in line. The Commons had inherited the seventeenth-century distrust of the executive, although suspicion was now directed against the ministers rather than the sovereign personally. Until the middle of the century the majority of members, independent country gentlemen, acted as if it were their obligation to resist all ministerial influence and to try to establish by law the independence of the House—to break the working connection between ministers and the Commons that was growing stronger year by year. Attempts to achieve this separation had been written into the Act of Settlement of 1701, and although the crucial clause totally prohibiting all officeholders from sitting in the House of Commons was soon radically modified, "place bills" of a similar sweeping character were repeatedly introduced and almost invariably passed by the House for the next forty years. Even in the second half of the century, this attitude of automatic suspicion of any government remained strong, and any politician in opposition could usually count on a favorable hearing for charges of ministerial corruption and undue influence. John Dunning's resolution of 1780 "that the influence of the Crown has increased, is increasing, and ought to be diminished" could pass, even though many who voted for it refused now to support the subsequent attempts to diminish the undue influence they had just condemned.

The impulse toward opposition in the House did not create permanent instability and turn the Commons into an assembly as anarchic as the Polish Diet, since it was always weakened and sometimes completely incapacitated by quite contradictory attitudes in the minds of the very same men who distrusted every ministry on principle. Most of them, except those extreme Tories with strong Jacobite sympathies in the decades immediately after 1714, were as loyal to the crown as they were certain that every placeman was corrupt, so that many of them in practice gave a general support to the king's government, just because it was his government. Moreover, they considered persistent opposition verging on treason. A striking example of this divided mind appears in the debate and division on William Pulteney's motion in 1740 for an address to the king to remove Sir Robert Walpole from his counsels forever. Far from unifying the widespread opposition to Sir Robert as Pulteney had anticipated, it was shattered completely. Large numbers of country gentlemen, who usually voted against the ministry, either abstained from the division or actually voted with the government on the grounds that, reprehensible as Sir Robert was, he was still the king's minister and that sort of pressure on the king was presumptuous to the point of disloyalty. Thus Walpole owed one of his greatest victories more to his opponents than to the fruits of twenty years' exploitation of every means of government patronage and influence.

The independents would frequently withhold active support from government, but many of them would not regularly vote against ministers either, except on place bills or measures that touched their pockets directly. And even here, although they normally opposed taxation, ministers could usually appeal successfully to their patriotism for taxes, once a war had actually begun. But their support was always uncertain; it might be lost at any time by a blunder, an unsuccessful war, or even (despite the Pulteney example of 1740) a sustained Opposition campaign. Any minister could count on their support only by continued success and a willingness to bow to their prejudices—as Sir Robert Walpole had to do in the excise crisis in 1733 (see page 115) and in his refusal to press for further religious toleration, as George II, Newcastle, and Fox had to do in accepting Pitt as Secretary of State in 1757; and as George III had to do in ending the American war. If the Commons had been composed wholly of this sort of independent, apolitical member—and to extend their number was the object of most of the early agitation for parliamentary reform—the task of governing would have been nearly impossible. Fortunately, they were not the only type of men in the House, and it was among the other members that a dependable working majority could be, and was, established.

Independent country gentlemen, always tending to opposition, composed a numerical majority of the House, but a considerable number of members stood at the opposite pole, enthusiastically supporting any ministry that the king approved. Contemporaries usually called them the "permanent Court party" or the "Court and Treasury party." Estimates of the size of this group vary from decade to decade, and inevitably depend on arbitrary decisions as to whether particular individuals could be influenced by any political loyalty other than their attachment to their office. But with all due allowance for doubtful cases, it normally included about one hundred members, most of whom attended debates faithfully (especially those debates likely to produce a critical division), and they voted with the administration regardless of its composition. Their loyalty was to ministers as ministers, not to any individual or connection except to the king himself.

Professional and semiprofessional administrators and courtiers formed the core of the Court and Treasury group. Some of the former were already essentially civil servants, permanently in an office below the cabinet level and providing the administrative continuity for the more important government departments. Philip Stephens was a typical figure: M.P. for Sandwich from 1768 to 1806, and Secretary of the Admiralty from 1763 to 1795, through the Grenville, Rockingham, Chatham, Grafton, North, Rockingham, Shelburne, Coalition, and Pitt administrations—a man essentially outside of politics. Others were more politically oriented, at least for a part of their careers, but still primarily administrators, willing to fill any of the secondary offices for virtually any administration. The second Viscount Barrington (an Irish Peer), an M.P. from 1740 to 1778, was variously a Lord of the Admiralty under Henry

?elham, Chancellor of the Exchequer for a few months in 1761–
762, then Treasurer of the Navy from 1762 to 1765, and finally
;ecretary-at-War in the Rockingham administration. Here he
ound a permanent niche where he remained for thirteen years
ınder Rockingham, Chatham, Grafton, and North. Like Ste-
ɔhens, his allegiance was to office rather than to a politician or
. political connection, but he was rather closer to time-serving
han was Stephens. Since all of his offices were basically political
.ppointments, normally changing hands with major changes in
.dministration, his tenure of them depended upon his shifting
ɔolitical loyalties.

The "professional" courtiers were a less numerous group
n the Commons than the administrators, but there were always
ome of them. Most of the really lucrative or prestigous court
ɔffices were political plums, but there were a host of lesser ones,
`eal or nominal, staffed by men whose whole lives centered on
he Royal Household, and who thought of themselves as per-
onally dependent on the king. If they sat in Parliament (only
ı fraction of them did), they considered it part of their duty
o support his ministry as long as the king himself did. The
Honorable James Brudenell, younger son of a major aristocratic
amily whose every member sought a court office, and master of
he robes to George III for thirty-two years, was an M.P. from
.754 until he was rewarded with a peerage in 1780. According
o the duke of Newcastle, who at first considered him so close a
ɔersonal friend that he returned him to Parliament on his pri-
ʌate interest in 1761, Brudenell wrote to Bute shortly after New-
:astle's resignation promising to support the new ministry's
measures, without knowing or inquiring what they were to be.
He subsequently supported every other ministry during his
ɔarliamentary career through five major changes of administration.

The bulk of the Court and Treasury group, however, were
ɔf a still different sort from the administrators and courtiers.
They were the M.P.'s looking for an undemanding office or
sinecure or some other income from the government for themselves or their families—or in other cases hoping for an honor,
usually a peerage. Their support shifted with every ministerial

change until their desire was fulfilled. Even then their loyalty was directed at the king, or the office, rather than at the individual minister who had gratified them, because some new prize had glittered on their horizon which could only be given by the government—any government. The last two sorts, courtiers and office or honor seekers, were numerous in the peerage; there were indeed so many that a majority of the House of Lords could usually be described as members of the Court and Treasury group. As a result, their immediate family connections and dependents in the Commons could often be treated as permanent "Ins" as well. A number of the smaller family groups in politics such as the Brudenells, were of this type.

Beyond the professional place-hunters, the composition of the Court and Treasury group shaded off into other groups and individuals in the House—the numerous men who were in Parliament primarily to promote their business or professional interests. Most of the merchants and many of the lawyers and military and naval officers were ordinarily indistinguishable in their political conduct from the hard-core Court and Treasury men. There were usually a few "moneyed men" connected with Opposition at any time and a rather more numerous group of lawyers and high officers trying to speed up their advancement by making a nuisance of themselves so that the ministry would meet their prices quickly. But the majority acted on the principle that the surest route to preferment was through steady loyalty to the present holders of power, and those who opposed for a time were nearly always ready to make a private bargain with any administration ready to gratify them.

Because so many members of Parliament felt no loyalty to anything but their quest for office, or for security in it, any set of ministers who enjoyed the royal confidence could count on a parliamentary base of about a hundred certain votes and perhaps fifty more that were likely to be given to them consistently by the very fact that they were in office, regardless of who they were. They would lose these votes, or find them unreliable, only when they were obviously tottering in royal favor or in the confidence of the independent country gentlemen. In that case, normally "safe" members might begin to absent themselves from crucial divisions, abstain from voting, or even (more rarely) vote against the ministry in the hope of securing their own futures with the successors to the incumbent ministers. This sort of desertion plagued the last months of Sir Robert Walpole's ministry, when several members who had always supported him developed dubious illnesses or had to go on pressing business out of London. The first Rockingham ministry was never sure of any of the Court and Treasury votes, not only because the king himself obviously considered its ministers merely as the lesser evil of the moment, but also because the Rockinghams did not have a wide base of support from either the independents or the active politicians in Parliament. At the same time, regular support of the Court and Treasury group, although essential to the life of a ministry, was never ultimately decisive in its continued success or even its very existence. The majority of these members and their satellites were silent votes, and every ministry needed more than votes to survive.

What was really decisive for the life and security of a ministry was obtaining the votes of the largest possible number of the more politically active members of the House, who usually numbered between 100 and 150 and comprised the overwhelming majority of talent in the Commons—men who had the essential debating strength to explain and defend ministerial policy and actions against the suspicions of the independents and the attacks of Opposition orators. They possessed the administrative talents to staff the ministry, occasionally at the cabinet level (although these posts were more likely to be filled by peers) but particularly in the offices of secondary rank, such as the junior lords of the Treasury and Admiralty or the Paymaster of the Army. The initial construction of the ministry was designed to obtain the support of as many as possible of these able politicians. Since most ministries of the century were coalitions of several political and family groups, important offices were distributed to include from each group as many men with pretensions to place as possible. Those ministries that were truly comprehensive—Henry Pelham's after 1746, the Newcastle-Pitt-Fox coalition of 1757, and Lord North's ministry for most of its life—encountered little effective opposition, because an overwhelming majority of political talent belonged to the administration. In contrast, ministries formed of essentially one group, or coalitions that excluded too many active and ambitious individuals and smaller connections, had a very difficult time. Sir Robert Walpole (despite his numerical majority) was never really easy in Parliament after the excise crisis of 1733 because he had excluded or alienated too many talented, active politicians; they could not drive him from office because they were too divided among themselves, but they were strong enough to make every session an unpleasant struggle. The instability of the four years between his fall and the Pelhams' consolidation of power in 1746 arose from the series of imperfect coalitions between the "Old Corps" of Walpoleans and the various other groups; and the attempts between 1754 and 1757 to construct ministries on the basis of only one or two of the three major connections of these years all failed.

The underlying reasons for the instability of ministries in the first decade of George III's reign was a series of similar attempts by individual groups or partial coalitions to govern, excluding too many other active politicians. In these years particularly, when medium-sized connections were numerous (Rockinghams, Grenvilles, Bedfords, Chathamites) and reasonably coherent, the attempt to break the connections and to construct ministries, if possible, of individuals detached from each of them—as George III hoped to do—was inevitably doomed to failure; too many pretensions were bound to be left unsatisfied. The same failure to form an adequate coalition and then the creation of an unpopular one between the archantagonists Fox and North were also contributing causes to the troubles of 1782–1784. (See pages 149–155.) The secret of a long-lived, stable administration was the construction of a broadly inclusive ministry, incorporating the largest possible number of politically active members in the House.

Sustaining a Ministry

INFLUENCE AND PATRONAGE The establishment of a broad base of support for an administration at the beginning of its tenure did not guarantee survival. That could only be secured by rewarding the original supporters for past services and en-

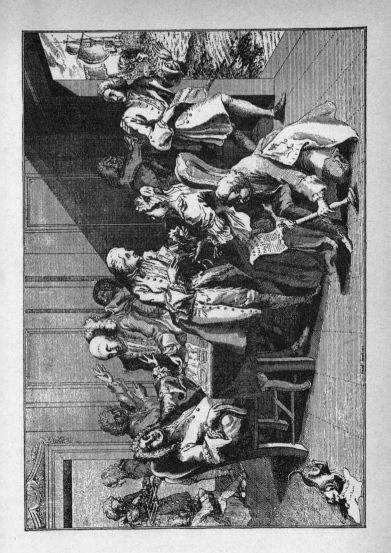

"In Place." A satire of 1738 attacking Walpole's "corruption" and "subservience to Spain." *(New York Public Library)*

couraging further ones. New recruits had to be won from individuals and groups omitted in the original scheme, from among the independents, and from new members returned at elections. It was here—in maintaining and extending the ministerial majority—that the use of influence, vital to the day-by-day operations of politics, was developed into a fine art. The three major groups in Parliament—the independents, the Court and Treasury types, and the active politicians—all required different techniques of management. So did each individual member of these groups. The politician who could master the largest number of techniques, the most detailed knowledge of every form of patronage, and relate them to the desires of specific individuals succeeded best. Sir Robert Walpole and the Duke of Newcastle survived as long as they did because of their intimate knowledge of individuals within and without Parliament, of the possibilities for manipulation of the administrative system, and of the state of the various competing interests in every county and borough not subject to absolute nomination by a patron. The remark attributed to Sir Robert that "every member has his price, and I know it," was a boast of his command of this sort of knowledge, not merely a cynical comment on his fellow members; the mountain of Newcastle's correspondence (more than 300 folio volumes) is a monument to a similar command of the multitudinous details of parliamentary management. Every vacancy in state and church, from top to bottom, might well be used to gratify some old ally or win a new one or shift the balance of interests in a borough into friendly hands. If misused, it added a new vote to Opposition.

The ministers who failed, such as Carteret, Bute, and Grenville, were all singularly deficient in this sort of knowledge and attention to the details of patronage and management. Carteret, an extremely able diplomatist with a greater command of European politics than any other Englishman of his time and a personal favorite of George II, had nothing but contempt for the management of the House of Commons, and hence was without influence or even respect there. Bute, a pure courtier until George III made him principal minister, was almost as completely ignorant of English politics in every particular as was

George himself, and the two had to submit to the ignominy of calling in Henry Fox, whom they rightly considered the most notoriously corrupt of all the politicians, to conduct the preliminaries of the Peace of Paris through Parliament. Indeed, it was Bute's awareness of his own inadequacies as a manipulator of influence as much as timidity that led him to resign from office—and it was the king's growing sense that this sort of management was essential to political control that brought him to dispense with Bute altogether and then to become himself something of the true successor of Walpole and Newcastle in his attention to political detail. George Grenville too, it seemed, was never able to master the use of patronage and influence to win support, although he tried. His correspondence shows him repeatedly offending his colleagues and supporters by his ignorance and indecision over appointments.

The essence of effective ministerial management lay in the judicious distribution of all the forms of patronage at the chief minister's disposal: the many hundreds of offices, efficient and nominal, in the administration and at court, descending from cabinet posts through customs places in decayed seaports down to footmen in the Royal Household. If these offices were important or lucrative enough, they went first to members themselves, then to their families and dependents; lesser places were distributed to their constituents and connections of constituents. Preferments in the church and crown livings for younger sons, old tutors, and miscellaneous connections rewarded other members. The earls of Cardigan and Northumberland repeatedly promised their own and their dependents' unswerving support to several ministers in return for dukedoms. Other honors and titles—decorations, knighthoods, baronetcies and Irish peerages—bought scores of other members. Contracts and favorable terms on loans attracted the votes and support of financiers and rich merchants. Military rewards, diplomatic appointments, recommendations to the East India Company, favors for constituents who had business with one of the government departments—whatever, in short, was likely to encourage a regular supporter or win a new adherent—were used to secure votes. As Henry Fox wrote to Horace Walpole on offering the rangership of St. James's and Hyde Parks to Walpole's nephew, Lord Orford, "If he does choose it, I doubt not of his and his friend Boone's hearty assistance, and believe I shall see you, too, much oftener in the House of Commons. This is offering you a bribe, but 'tis such a one as one honest good-natured man may without offence offer to another."[1] George Bubb Dodington, place-hunter extraordinary, summed up the whole system: "Service implies obligation and obligation implies return."

Ministers might offer everything, except the direct purchase of votes. Despite the many contemporary charges, there is no evidence that parliamentary votes were ever purchased for cash across the board in the eighteenth century as had happened at times in the seventeenth. Certainly the active politicians were above suspicion of this sort of crude bribery. Guineas were reserved for nursing boroughs and getting into Parliament in the first place. Office or its equivalent was the inducement—although the grant of a lucrative sinecure is not always distinguishable from a bag of gold. Still, contemporaries had a fairly clear idea of what were strictly legitimate forms of influence and what was corruption—a distinction drawn much more sharply when one was in opposition than when one was in office.

Contemporary stories of numerous "secret pensions" and large-scale payments from the secret service fund of the crown to members of Parliament are fictitious. Some areas of possible cash transactions, the Irish pension lists and pensions granted on various branches of the customs, have not been as thoroughly investigated as the surviving accounts of secret service money, and may still conceal some secrets. Virtually nothing is known about possible English uses of the Hanoverian revenues of the kings, at which an occasional contemporary hinted darkly. But from what is known, pensions and other money payments made to members from secret service money or other revenues fall into several quite definite and harmless categories. Many of the largest regular payments were to ministers themselves, intended as supplements for the inadequate salaries attached to

---

[1] Horace Walpole, *Correspondence,* ed. W. S. Lewis, New Haven, 1937– XXX, 167–168.

some of the major offices of state. Most of the other large pensions were granted on a temporary basis until an office was available or a promised reversion (a legal promise of the right of succession to an office) fell in. Lord Holderness received a pension of £4000 a year until the position of Lord Warden of the Cinque Ports, which he had been promised for giving up the office of Secretary of State to Lord Bute, became vacant. It was also common form to grant a pension to any major politician, and to many of his dependents, upon his retirement. Finally a number of pensions were given to cases of real need among nonpolitical types such as impoverished Scottish peers or widowed gentlewomen. The remaining pensions to members—somewhere around a dozen in most surviving lists—were too few to have any significant effect on parliamentary majorities.

Government expenditures on elections were likewise grossly exaggerated. The king and ministers spent insignificant sums in relation to the total cost of an election, even to the expenses of single contested elections. The government normally spent between £25,000 and £50,000 on an entire general election; in the Oxfordshire contest of 1754 the two sides spent £40,000, and successive contests in Bristol in 1764 and 1765 absorbed £60,000. In the general election of 1761, once considered as an especially flagrant example, no crown money was spent, since George III put his original conception of political virtue into practice by refusing to authorize election expenditure out of secret service money. A few boroughs, where government influence had long been established, were carefully nursed by ministers; some government supporters received financial assistance toward supporting their private electoral interests; and the ministers acted as "brokers" between the great boroughmongers (mostly Cornish) and prospective candidates, but that was all. Had "influence" over either members or constituencies been a matter of the simple purchase of a majority of either members or constituencies at or immediately after an election, the task of ministers would have been much easier.

The largest single bloc of votes in the House was as unobtainable by the distribution of ordinary patronage as it was by direct bribery—the votes of the some 250 independent country gentlemen sitting on their own interest for boroughs or by the suffrages of their social equals for the counties. Many of them had to be written off completely, as they were in permanent, apolitical opposition to government as such, unreachable by any appeal of any ministry, and the others could be counted on only for the first few months of a ministry's life. After that, only an efficient conduct of ordinary administration at home, the maintainence of British interests abroad, attention to their prejudices in favor of low taxes, no meddling with the religious establishment, and generally leaving things exactly as they were could maintain their support. The country gentlemen rarely wanted anything for themselves other than recognition of their local importance by appointments as justices of the peace or commissioners of the land tax. When Henry Pelham started granting these appointments to any gentleman of local promi- nence, abandoning Walpole's policy of distinguishing between professed "Whigs" and reputed "Tories," the majority of coun- try gentlemen began to support rather than oppose government. A country gentleman who usually voted with the government might occasionally ask a favor for a son or dependent: a commis- sion in the army or navy, a crown living in the church, or (to- ward the end of the century) a recommendation to the East India Company. He might even request a little ministerial pressure in his constituency if he was challenged by someone openly con- nected with Opposition. But he would rarely ask for anything large enough to compromise his professed independence, and treated anything he obtained as a just recognition of his own local importance or a reward for past support. Nor in granting the occasional requests of the country gentlemen did the minis- ters assume that they were imposing obligations for future conduct. Only rarely could government hope to find a country gentleman ambitious enough or sufficiently distressed finan- cially to attach himself permanently to a political connection or the Court and Treasury interest.

Satisfying the members of the Court and Treasury group and augmenting their number demanded techniques quite dif- ferent from those required to cultivate the approval of the country gentlemen. During the course of a long ministry, the

members who supported it for places alone always became confused with the personal connections of ministers who were
supporting it out of loyalty to their chiefs as individuals rather
than as the temporary tenants of office. These personal followers,
when rewarded with court appointments, sinecures, or even
efficient offices, might well become detached from their old
loyalties and develop a new one to the king, to their office, or
even (if the places were for life) develop a real independence
of conduct. Andrew Stone, Newcastle's private secretary and
confidant, who was generously rewarded by his patron, refused
to give up his sinecures and follow his master into opposition.
At the same time officeholders inherited from previous administrations who had shifted their loyalty to the new ministry rather
than lose their places might be converted into personal followers either through gratification of their particular ambition or
through the growth of private friendship with one of the new
ministers. The personal connections that a fallen minister took
with him into opposition were usually quite different from those
he had brought in with him, or had counted as personal adherents while in office.

It was by no means the case, as Burke asserted, that a
"party" always left office smaller than it had been when it came
in because its "weaker" members had been tempted away by
places. He was only generalizing from the particular circumstances of the first Rockingham administration, which had lost
some of its original adherents in 1766 to Chatham's new administration, most notably General Conway, the Secretary of State.
He was probably thinking too of Newcastle's disappointment in
1762 when so many men whom the duke had thought his own
made their peace with Bute and Fox. But the only other parallel
case occurred in 1782 when the Foxite group resigned after
Rockingham's death, and several prominent members of the
original connection, including Conway again and the duke of
Richmond, remained in office under Shelburne. George Grenville, however, left office in 1765 with a sizable personal connection, although he had no following at all when he became principal minister in 1763, and his group retained its integrity as a
major "party" until its leader began to lose interest in politics

shortly before his death. Lord North also acquired enough of a personal following during his ministry to make his connection in the two years after his fall in 1782 the largest single group in Parliament, although many of these men quickly reverted to the younger Pitt after the destruction of the Fox-North coalition. Even so, both Grenville and North had created a political connection out of members who seemed at first sight Court and Treasury types.

But the basic problem a minister faced was not to create a personal following out of men inclined to support all administrations in the pursuit of their private ends. It was to ensure their undeviating loyalty for the time being, and this was best done by gratifying them as far as possible with what they wanted, and making it clear that the patronage distributed came to them directly through ministerial hands. Here, as with the active politicians, unequivocal royal support was essential to the principal minister for effective control of the House. The king's explicit consent was necessary for most appointments of any importance, and the first three Georges all insisted on being consulted about every one of them. Whatever patronage was attached to office as such, apart from the Treasury (where many of the lesser revenue offices were in the First Lord's immediate gift), was slight and jealously guarded by the incumbent for his personal use. Since the disposal of most patronage was at the discretion of the king, a minister was counted powerful in direct relation to how far the king followed his recommendations and how clearly it was seen that it was his candidates who got the appointments, promotions, honors, and contracts they sought, and not the candidates of some potential rival in the Cabinet Council or at court, or worse still, the protégé of some recently displaced minister.

The "rats" who abandoned Sir Robert Walpole in droves for Sir Spencer Compton at the accession of George II did a rapid *volte-face* when the new king accepted several of Walpole's candidates over other claimants. The running battle between the Pelhams and Carteret between 1742 and 1746 revolved around patronage as much as it did around disagreements on foreign policy. Henry Fox refused to serve under Newcastle in

1754 when the duke made it clear that he intended to reserve the disposal of all patronage for himself, although Fox was to have been minister for the House of Commons and intended to use the position to increase his own following. George Grenville offended the king personally by his insistence on absolute control of patronage, and indeed the whole myth of "secret influence" was based in part on George III's readiness to appoint candidates other than those pressed on him by his ministers. He particularly resented the attempt of the Fox-North coalition to obtain complete control over patronage as the price of accepting office in 1783, and even when he was forced to surrender, he made an ostentatious display of his umbrage by refusing to create any new peers.

Even when the channels for the distribution of patronage were perfectly evident, there were many real problems in dealing with the claims and desires of the relatively sure supporters of any stable ministry. What these men wanted all too often conflicted with the demands of some less committed member, whose vote might be permanently won or lost by gratification. One frequent way of dealing with conflicting claims of this kind was to give the immediate opening to the doubtful member and a reversion to the same office, or to some other place, to the man already supporting the ministry. Samuel Martin, Secretary of the Treasury, who played a discreditable role in the early stages of the Wilkes affair in 1763, was further rewarded with the reversion to one of Horace Walpole's life places, and caused the latter a good deal of amusement by his assiduous enquiries after his health during Walpole's attacks of the gout. Although reversions were rarely given for any of the more "efficient" offices, they multiplied among the sinecure places until some of them were committed for two or three lives, and because reversions were regarded as a species of property, they slowed down the pace of administrative reform at the end of the century.

A formal reversion was a legal commitment that many ministers avoided when they could in dealing with men whose support they did not doubt. They preferred to get by with a mere promise of the next vacancy or "something equivalent soon," and the really assiduous courters of all administrations showed a remarkable willingness to be fobbed off repeatedly without going into opposition. Lord Conyngham, an Irish peer who was M.P. for Sandwich 1756–1774 and who had considerable parliamentary influence in Ireland, had been twice disappointed by Grenville in the summer and fall of 1763 in requests for places, first for a friend and then for his nephew and heir. He wrote an angry letter announcing that he had "not the disposition either of a minister or a courtier" and was to be put down in opposition to the government.[2] But there is no evidence that he ever voted against government, and indirect evidence that he supported it in crucial divisions a few months later. When another request for an appointment for a protégé was granted in February 1765, he repledged himself to Grenville, and in June was asking for the office of Master-General of the Irish Ordnance for himself. Their last exchange was a few days later, on the eve of Grenville's dismissal, when Conyngham asked Grenville who the new ministry's Lord Lieutenant would be, so that he could apply to him instead for the coveted office. His one political principle was an indiscriminate support of every administration for his own ends.

Even the Conynghams could not be staved off indefinitely, and the temporary piques of this sort of member were always annoying and at times dangerous. Intrigues at court and within ministries abounded, ranging from such fateful conflicts as that between Oxford and Bolingbroke, which ruined the Tories in 1714, down to insignificant squabbles concerning which lady of the bedchamber should pass the queen her basin to wash her hands. Apparently minor desertions could be disastrous when a ministry was in trouble, as Sir Robert Walpole discovered in 1742. The duke of Dorset, a typical courtier who had long dabbled in petty intrigues against the minister, decided to embark briefly upon open opposition for no discernable reason. Dorset's three sons in the House of Commons thereupon voted against Sir Robert in divisions where every vote counted and in which

[2] *Additional Grenville Papers,* ed. J. R. G. Tomlinson, Manchester University Press, 1962, p. 63.

other "safe" members were beginning to abstain. Sir Robert, however, was a master at judging how far such intrigues were likely to go, and whether their instigators were best ignored, had to be rewarded, or deserved discipline. This quality was in striking contrast to Newcastle's neurotic anxiety to placate members whom it would have been difficult to offend in any case. He never quite understood that many members were easily managed and brought into line, unless the government was obviously slipping in the royal confidence or in its command of an effective majority in the House of Commons.

The management of the politically able and ambitious members was a far more acute problem than keeping the country gentlemen happy or the Court and Treasury types contented. The price of their initial support was far higher, and their loyalty to a principal minister was far harder to maintain over a prolonged period, for all of them were his potential rivals. The formation of the ministry itself, always a coalition of several competing interests whose members were frequently in search of the same office, usually left a reservoir of ill-will somewhere in the heart of the administration. All pretensions could never be met, and a good many posts usually had to be reserved for holdovers from the previous ministry who wanted to stay on. One of the causes of the instability between 1742 and 1746 was the relatively few offices available to distribute to the new groups whom it was necessary to attach to the "Old Corps." Moreover, the king and the old ministers were determined to give most of the new recruits only the appearance, not the reality, of an important voice in the ministry.

Covert rivalries within the cabinet between members of various parts of the original coalition were not the only causes of internal dissension. Men once intimately associated with each other in the early stages of a ministry and closely related by blood or marriage might contend for primacy. Walpole and Townshend, brothers-in-law, after intriguing together against Stanhope and Sunderland between 1714 and 1722, fell out themselves in the later 1720s, not only because they disagreed on foreign policy, but also because Townshend resented being upstaged by his once junior partner—and indeed Walpole eventually collided with most of his really able associates. Henry Pelham and his brother the duke of Newcastle were sometimes not on speaking terms even at the height of their joint struggle with Carteret for supremacy in the cabinet, and Pelham always had as much trouble in pacifying the duke as he did in neutralizing men in open opposition. Ministries frequently contained the seeds of their own dissolution through rivalries between their more prominent members.

Another source of internal stress within a ministry was its supporters, sometimes even in high office, who had ambitions beyond their ability and who felt they had been relegated to inferior posts. They continually chafed at imagined slights, readily exacerbated differences among the more able members of administration, and even broadcast their dissatisfaction by a speech or vote in Parliament. Earl Temple and the fourth Viscount Townshend were particularly difficult men of this stamp during the middle decades of the century; their constant resentment at imagined "neglect" was serious because of Temple's influence on his relatives, including the elder Pitt, and Townshend's on his unstable but brilliant brother Charles, whom every ministry courted. The younger Pitt had similar trouble with his cousin the marquis of Buckingham who, like his uncle Lord Temple, had an overexalted opinion of his own abilities and his claims upon his relatives, the government, and the king. Every major minister was tormented at one time or another, and frequently continuously, with trying to keep his original supporters happy.

A minister could sometimes deal with the discontents of his supporters by shifts in offices and in the higher court appointments, so that all ministries were repeatedly rearranged in the attempt to preserve harmony. An efficient office could be opened to a man of real talent by persuading its holder to accept a more prestigious but empty court appointment, especially if he was incompetent at actual business, as several of the more politically important peers were. At other times, a discontented officeholder might consent to remain where he was, provided that he received a personal summons to the cabinet to which his office alone did not entitle him, as was done for the earl of Halifax, the First Lord of Trade, in 1757, and for various commoners who held the office of Chancellor of the Exchequer when the First Lord of the Treasury was a peer. A cabinet invitation, however, was considered an extraordinary concession, and attempts at mollification more often took the form of a peerage or a promotion or an honor for himself or a relative.

Nevertheless, the chief minister was repeatedly faced with decisions on whether discontented men within the administration were worth placating or whether they were expendable: How far must they be allowed some latitude to pursue their own ends? How essential was their support and that of their connections? When and how should they be disciplined? Serious divisions of opinion on foreign policy for example, especially when accompanied by mutual jealousies and strong demands for places and power, usually led to dismissal or resignation, as when the Bedfords quitted the Pelham ministry in 1751. But most ministers preferred to work out an accommodation rather than to increase the opposition. Sir Robert Walpole was alone in his readiness to discipline defectors by dismissal—not only single individuals such as William Pulteney from the cofferership of the Household in 1725 and Pitt from his cornetcy of the horse in 1736 for an opposition speech in Parliament, but wholesale punishments such as were meted out to former supporters who opposed the Excise Bill in 1733, when seven peers, including Chesterfield and Cobham, lost either their offices or their regiments. Normally, however, a consistent opposition, not an occasional isolated instance, was required before a man would be dismissed from even a clearly political place, and the punishment of political waywardness by cashiering a military officer was considered scandalous, as the furor which surrounded General Conway's dismissal for voting against the government in the Wilkes affair in 1764 indicated. A clean sweep, or anything approaching it, even at a major change of administration was unusual, and more energy was spent in trying to persuade members of the former ministry to remain in office than was expended in trying to root out all its supporters. The supposed "massacre of the Pelhamite innocents" in 1762–1763, which Newcastle represented as the wholesale dismissal of all his appointees for the past twenty years, actually involved only a few dozen individuals who openly refused to support the duke's successors. The Rockinghamite demand to reconstruct the ministry completely, if they were to come into office, was considered most irregular, if not actually unconstitutional, by most contemporaries. There were definite limits beyond which discipline for defection did not go. Attempts to meet the demands of the discontented were most common. At worst they were allowed to execute their threats of resignation when it seemed evident that the administration could survive without them, or that their vacated places could be used to conciliate some other unrest within the administration or be used as lures for important new recruits from outside.

Another vital ministerial task was extending the base of the government by enticing politicians and their connections out of opposition into an alliance with the administration. All ministries were reconstructed as new men and even whole groups were brought into office. It was the ideal way of dealing with an exceptionally strong opposition orator or bloc of opposition votes, and a highly practicable one when the active part of opposition consisted of a coalition like the administration, and differed from the ministry by being out of office, not by disagreement on policy and principles. There was scarcely a year in the eighteenth century when ministers were not attempting to negotiate a union with their ostensible rivals in opposition, and at times these attempted coalitions became the chief activity of the politicians. Sometimes the principal ministers even willfully ignored or affronted their colleagues so that some of them would resign, leaving places to buy off professed opponents who seemed more valuable. The death of a prominent politician, which might open several places and make possible a general rearrangement involving a dozen or more shifts, would provide the opportunity for acquiring new supporters. The duke of Newcastle's correspondence sometimes assumes a ghoulish tone in his speculations on what could be done as the result of an expected death.

Joint appointment to minor but lucrative posts such as Postmaster-General, Vice-Chamberlain of the Household, and

Vice-Treasurer of Ireland, also created new places to offer politicians. The replacement of single great officers of state by boards, begun in the seventeenth century and turned into standard practice in the eighteenth for the Treasury and Admiralty, resulted as much from a need to multiply offices for members of Parliament as it did from fears of overmighty ministers and administrative efficiency. Very few wholly new offices worth a member's acceptance were created, however. The more valuable posts of revenue commissioner, for example, were made incompatible with a seat in Parliament—although these could be used as a dumping ground for former officeholders or as a reward for a member's brother or son. Reforms and expansion in the Treasury, especially in the customs and excise, also provided a good deal of minor patronage, unavailable earlier, which could be used to court a member's constituents. These reforms also completed the process by which many of the older offices in the financial system had long been turning into sinecures, and made them more useful than they had formerly been as political bait for members.

Patronage was also extended far beyond appointments to places, real or nominal, in the administration. For the first time the church was completely exploited as a field of political patronage. All the valuable places were filled by relatives and friends of politicians. Only the constant vigilance of the kings kept the army and navy from being brought more completely into the system than they were. Posts in the colonies, too, which could be administered by deputy, were used to attract politicians, and as English control in India expanded and the East India Company became more dependent on the government, still another rich field of patronage opened up. The object of ministers was always to find something that would turn critics into supporters.

Nevertheless, patronage was rarely as calculatingly used as it might have been. Most ministers were fully as concerned to serve themselves, their families, dependents, personal friends, and connections at the public expense as they were to acquire votes in Parliament, and they bestowed the richest plums on these groups rather than used them to allure new support. The largest sinecures were given to the children or other close relatives of the principal minister. Sir Robert Walpole made his eldest son Auditor of the Exchequer, worth at least £7000 or £8000 a year, and on the second Lord Orford's death, he was succeeded by the earl of Lincoln, Newcastle's nephew, who was already Joint Comptroller of the Customs of London. Sir Robert's second son, Edward, was Master of the Pleas and Escheats and Clerk of the Pells in the Exchequer, and his youngest son, Horace, was Usher, Comptroller of the Pipe, and Clerk of the Estreats in the Exchequer. In addition, they shared a Collectorship in the Customs and some minor places. Such a concentration of places was common; those who already had a place, and the ear of a minister, got another, so that the same members were rewarded again and again. Most of the major politicians served England adequately, but they served their families and friends even better.

CONDUCTING BUSINESS THROUGH PARLIAMENT Every ministry, in order to survive, had to be able to show a successful record in preserving stability at home and advancing English interests abroad as well as winning parliamentary votes by dispensing places and favors. The substance of administration was not patronage but national finance, foreign affairs, the protection and encouragement of English commerce, the proper maintenance of the army and navy, and at times the repression of disturbances. Sound schemes and their successful application, however, were not of themselves adequate to win support for ministers in Parliament, as Sir Robert Walpole found in the excise crisis and in his attempts to preserve the peace with Spain. The ministerial case had to be presented to Parliament and defended; influential public opinion had, if possible, to be conciliated, for it was usually antiministerial and easily inflamed by opposition attacks.

All this meant that much attention had to be paid to the organization of business for the parliamentary session: the prearrangement of debate as far as was possible and the subsidizing of the press and pamphlets. Inadequate preparation and presentation of the financial estimates for the year could bring a ministry into contempt, as happened in 1756 and again in 1762–1763, when Sir George Lyttelton and Sir Francis Dashwood, the Chancellors of the Exchequer, displayed almost total ignorance of finance. Horace Walpole described the former as having "stumbled over millions, and dwelt pompously upon farthings" in introducing his budget, and a few weeks later as never knowing "prices from duties, nor drawbacks from premiums."[3] In both cases, the ministries so ill served shortly collapsed. In the occasional full-dress debates in both Houses reviewing some question of foreign policy or an opposition motion of "no confidence" in the administration, an adequate defense of the previous course of action was essential for survival. The effective presentation of the government's case was a serious problem even in a House of Lords containing a half-dozen cabinet ministers. The majority of the peers were not orators: the duke of Newcastle was totally unimpressive, although at least a frequent speaker, and the marquis of Rockingham and the duke of Portland could hardly be persuaded to open their mouths, whether they were leading ministries or oppositions. As a result several peers were created with the sole purpose of leading debate in the Lords—Lord Hervey by Walpole to counter the oratory of Carteret and Chesterfield, Lord Grenville by the younger Pitt. The need for able debaters was even more acute in the House of Commons. When the principal minister was a peer, the selection of a "minister for the House of Commons" was crucial, and very rarely successfully resolved, which encouraged ambitious men to follow the precedent of Sir Robert Walpole and remain in the Lower House. All the long-lasting ministries of the second half of the century were led from the Commons—by Henry Pelham, the elder Pitt, Lord North, and the younger Pitt.

Even when the principal minister was in the Commons, the conduct of the government's case was a serious problem; in the absence of most of the other ministers of cabinet rank, a tremendous load fell on the first minister's shoulders. He might well find himself, as Walpole and both Pitts frequently did, hav-

[3] Horace Walpole, *Letters,* ed. Mrs. Paget Toynbee, London, 1903–1905, III, 389, 403.

ing to carry the full weight of debate on every facet of administration. Even under better circumstances, his lieutenants were
likely to be no more than second- or third-rank members of the
ministry or new young recruits who would not impress the
skeptical back-benchers, whereas the opposition contained an
array of the greatest orators and most skilled debaters in the
House.

The order of the government speakers was frequently prearranged for important debates, younger and weaker members
going first, with the better orators and the principal minister
reserving themselves for a later stage. The opening debate of
each session, on the king's speech outlining the government's
plans and defending what the ministry had done during the
previous recess, was particularly crucial. Whenever possible
the ministers found sympathetic independents or new recruits
to move and second approval of the king's speech and to carry
the burden of its defense. If a ministry felt really secure in its
majority, the more important members of administration might
well stand aside completely on this and similar ceremonial
occasions, giving the impression of overwhelming support for
themselves, since it was already a convention that the king's
messages were exclusively the work of his ministers. To carry
the Addresses of Thanks for them without a division, or to defeat
attempted opposition amendments overwhelmingly might even
discourage Opposition from attempting any concerted attack on
subsequent measures for the remainder of the session.

In the business of a session, there was very little to resemble
modern government programs. The closest parallels were the
annual financial measures, the infrequent necessity of obtaining
parliamentary approval for treaties with other powers, and
occasional miscellaneous bills and resolutions that the leaders
decided to treat as ministerial measures. An overwhelming
majority of the business at any time concerned private bills
(for turnpikes, river improvements and canals, local poor rates,
enclosures, modifying or breaking entails, divorces) or bills of
more general import which were not treated as government business and for which free debate and voting were allowed. Even if
a minister was deeply involved in such a measure, he felt no

need to resign if the bill was defeated or seriously amended. Members of the ministry and their regular supporters permitted themselves a great latitude of action. It was only in times of crisis that concerted attempts at party discipline were made, when supporters were instructed to attend and vote as the ministers wished, and when clear lines of divisions between the "Ins" and "Outs" could be detected.

The selection of the committees responsible for so much parliamentary business—especially the choice of their chairmen—was as important in the management of business as was the organization of debate. Most of the real discussion of bills took place in "committees of the whole," where proceedings were less formal than in Parliament proper (for instance, members could speak as often as they chose), so selection of temporary chairmen for these committees were occasions for political maneuvering. Opposition achieved several notable successes in advancing their cause at some stage of a particular bill by the election of a sympathetic chairman. Before Grenville's Election Act of 1770 effectively removed the adjudication of petitions about contested elections from politics by providing for their determination by select committees chosen by lot instead of by the entire House, the selection of the chairman of the grand committee on elections and privileges was crucial. This grand committee always decided contested elections along partisan lines, so the election of an unsympathetic chairman was, at best, a sign of an uncertain majority in the house. The defeat of Walpole's candidate for reelection in December 1741, Giles Earle, by four votes spelled Walpole's doom. The subsequent defeats that drove him to resignation were nearly all over election petitions, carried in favor of his opponents, which increased the number of opposition votes in the House and encouraged the increasing abstention of normal supporters who were ensuring their own futures.

The election of a sympathetic chairman of the committee on ways and means was vital too in getting the government's financial bills before the House without major mangling in committee, although the serious reverses that ministers sometimes suffered owed more to the occasional incompetence of the responsible ministers than to unsympathetic chairmen influencing the course of debate. The creation of important *ad hoc* committees on particular bills, for reviewing diplomatic negotiations, and later for dealing with problems of India, was also apt to be intensely political. There were repeated struggles to secure "select" rather than "secret" committees, or to have the committee elected by ballot rather than simply nominated by the government. The latter was sure to be weighted in favor of administration while in the former procedure the opposition could hope to insert some sympathetic neutrals if not, indeed, some of themselves. Occasionally two conflicting committees were set up, creating a situation that further complicated the problems under consideration. The already confused problems of India and the East India Company in the late 1770s and early 1780s were further confounded by the competition between the Select Committee dominated by the opposition, especially by Burke, and the Secret Committee dominated by Henry Dundas.

The Speaker of the House of Commons was still largely a political figure; his selection was usually the occasion for a trial of strength at the opening of a new Parliament or whenever a vacancy occurred in mid-course because the oppositon normally put up a candidate against the government's nominee and pressed their choice to a division. The important precedents for impartiality established by Arthur Onslow during his long Speakership (1727–1761) were much criticized by Walpole's adherents, and subsequent ministers sometimes suspected Onslow of flirting with Opposition. Lord North was seriously embarrassed when Sir Fletcher Norton, incensed by the government's legal promotions in 1780, openly joined the opposition, and replaced him with a more sympathetic member at the first opportunity. As late as 1790 Burke felt impelled to apologize to Sir Gilbert Elliot for not nominating him, even though the opposition had no hope of carrying him against the Pitt nominee, Henry Addington.

Ministers also had to conciliate politically important opinion inside and outside the House which could not be reached by ordinary forms of patronage. The most important groups with influence in politics were the country gentlemen and certain sections of the mercantile-commercial interest, par-

The House of Commons in Walpole's
Administration. Walpole talking to
Speaker Onslow. *(New York Public
Library)*

ticularly in London; but the number of politically conscious Englishmen was steadily growing, and as it did, the scope and types of government and opposition propaganda expanded and changed to appeal to this widening "political nation." The necessity of winning men by argument and performance forced ministers to select and frame their measures in ways likely to appeal to the uncommitted independents in the House and outside, and influenced the character and content of all parliamentary oratory. Ministers had at once to soothe the independents' suspicion of all politicians, appeal to their instinctive loyalty to the crown and to their patriotism, and convince them that the administration was doing the best possible job of promoting England's interests. A confirmed opponent could not be converted to give favorable votes, but an independent could be, especially if his fellows outside the House seemed to think well of the ministry. So a ministerial speech that was well received in the days before regular reporting of debates began to be tolerated (after 1774) might be revised and printed as a pamphlet to reach a wider audience—although Opposition was always much more active in the publication of parliamentary proceedings than were the ministers.

Much more common was the subsidizing of pamphlets and weekly newssheets stating the ministerial case and belittling the opposition, and increasingly in the latter half of the century, subsidizing as much of the growing daily and triweekly press as possible. Most administrations, however, were inept in their choice of propagandists and usually ill served by them. The ministries of William and Anne alone were well defended, enlisting at one time or another the support of Defoe, Swift, Addison, Steele, and even Locke. But after the Hanoverian succession the most brilliant pens usually served the opposition. Walpole's neglect of the press was notorious. His few literary sycophants were incompetent hacks, while Bolingbroke, Pulteney, and Chesterfield were writing against him in the *Craftsman,* Pope was satirizing him, and John Gay was ridiculing him in *The Beggar's Opera.* The same pattern continued in the latter half of the century. Burke, Junius (the anonymous author of letters attacking the ministry), even the authors of the *Rolliad* (a mock-epic attack on the younger Pitt in the 1780s), were more effective than the government pamphleteers. Ministers succeeded better with newspapers than they did with pamphlets, partly because they had greater resources with which to reward the publishers—not only financial grants, but access to information received from diplomats abroad. But even here, the papers sympathetic to Opposition tended to be better and more popular; too strong a government line alienated politically alert readers.

The later eighteenth-century ministers had better luck with still another technique for mobilizing, even for manufacturing, favorable opinion, a technique partly borrowed from Opposition experiments with petitioning movements and partly founded on the traditional practice of loyal and congratulatory addresses to the king on ceremonial occasions, military victories, and crises such as Jacobite uprisings. Organized campaigns of loyal addresses to the crown were employed with increasing effect from the outbreak of the American war onward; they helped to discredit the reform movement in 1780 and to create the impression of overwhelming support for Pitt prior to the general election of 1784 and during the regency crisis of 1788–1789. By the early years of the French Revolution, loyal addresses had become a major weapon in the government armory in attacking the opposition.

Ministers, of course, were rarely content merely to defend their policies and answer Opposition criticism; they naturally preferred to take the offensive and demolish their critics by representing them always as knaves and whenever possible as traitors. Until the 1720s a fallen minister or a vigorous opponent was always in some danger of losing his freedom and might even be threatened with the block. No politician was actually executed, but a number of them spent some time in the Tower. The incarceration of Walpole on charges of corruption in 1712 was revenged by the impeachment of Anne's last ministers in 1715. Sir Robert kept Bolingbroke excluded from the Lords, and was suspected of plotting more drastic action than dismissal against some of his other important critics—and they too threatened him with execution, although no one took them very seriously.

That sort of revenge was going out of fashion, and even contemplation. With the exception of Wilkes and Brass Crosby, no member of Parliament was imprisoned or expelled from the House for political opposition to a ministry after the 1740s. No action whatever was taken against the critics of the American war, and the worst thing that happened to any of the parliamentary opponents of the war with revolutionary France was the striking of Charles James Fox's name from the Privy Council in 1798, an empty punishment that had been occasionally applied earlier to intransigent opponents; it was similar to the dismissal of a peer from his lord lieutenancy for political opposition.

But if men in Opposition were quite safe in their persons, they were not necessarily so in their property and reputations. Their borough interests, in many instances conceived of as property, would of course be undermined as far as possible. Even more direct attacks were sometimes made. Men in Opposition who held places for life might find their salaries delayed — Horace Walpole complained that Henry Fox stopped his payments in 1763 for not voting for the preliminaries of peace, even though he had not voted against them. More serious was the attempt to rescind some of the crown grants originally made to Hans Bentinck in Cumberland in order to damage the financial and electoral interests of his descendant, the duke of Portland, a prominent opposition peer. This sort of economic threat seemed serious enough to the landed classes, most of whom held property once in the possession of the crown, to occasion the Nullum Tempus Act of 1769, which the government did not dare to oppose, terminating dormant claims by the crown after 60 years. But again, this sort of crude attack on a man's property for opposition was exceptional.

The reputation of a man in Opposition, however, was always fair game. The great "Whig" families rose to power in 1714 and remained there securely until 1760 by persuading first George I and then his son that the "Tories" of Anne's last ministry, ministers and supporters alike to the third and fourth generations, were all Jacobites. Sir Robert Walpole was particularly assiduous in cultivating this opinion, which had a substantial foundation until the late 1740s, and all the ministers until the accession of George III, except Pitt, did their best to equate opposition and even independence with Stuart sympathies. Such charges, of course, did not really work with displaced politicians who were excluded because they had quarreled with Walpole or the Pelhams, although it was regularly implied (occasionally with good reason) that they were doing the Jacobites' work for them out of resentment. Ministers could appeal also with some success to the still widespread feeling that opposition, at least "formed opposition," to the king's government was in some way disloyal. Most successful, however, in discrediting vocal opponents before 1760, because it was so close to the truth, was to represent their attacks as factious and interested, aimed at the ministers' places, not at their policies. This approach was particularly useful in encouraging division and dissension within the opposition, for the independent country gentlemen always doubted the sincerity and objectives of the opposition orators—as well they might, for each opposition politician was primarily concerned to make his own deal with the ministers, not to advance what the independents considered their own interests.

The attempt to discredit Opposition by innuendo and slander continued in the second half of the century, although the content changed. The charges that opposition was purely factious, of course, remained the stock in trade of ministerial supporters throughout the century and indeed opposition politicians often seemed as exclusively concerned with obtaining places as they had been earlier in the century. Nevertheless the increasing importance of issues after the accession of George III offered new lines for attack. While opposition orators were charging the ministers with arbitrary designs on the constitution, they were accused of meditating aristocratic schemes to enslave king and country in the interest of a few great families. When some members in opposition began to dabble in radical movements, all of them were represented as democrats and revolutionaries, a charge that had some effect in the crisis of 1779–1784 (see pages 141–155) and was extremely effective after 1792. Opposition's sympathy with the Americans could be, and was, interpreted as encouraging treason, especially after the war began in 1775; the charge became still more useful after France joined the war in 1778. From 1792 onward, members who opposed the war with France and continued to champion reform at home could be accused of disloyalty and revolutionary intentions.

All of these ministerial lines of attack often succeeded in discrediting Opposition because the men out of office so frequently played into Administration's hands by factious or grossly self-interested behavior and rhetorical excesses. Added to the popular prejudice against "formed opposition" to the king's government and the enormous resources of patronage and influence at the ministers' command, they helped to stack the deck against critics of government in normal times. Men who administered well, avoiding serious blunders at home and abroad, could usually expect to carry their measures by substantial majorities and to win their carefully prepared general elections by comfortable margins. But none of them succeeded in maintaining themselves in office indefinitely. Overconfidence, death, accident, miscalculations of sentiment, simple mistakes, extraneous circumstances, new issues, new men, might intervene at any time to swing the opinion of the independents and the king himself against them and bring their rivals to office. Opposition, unpopular and ineffectual as it often was, always ended by overturning even the most securely based and stable ministry.

CHAPTER FOUR

Opposition and the Growth of Parties

"Party is the madness of many for the gain of a few," proclaimed a pamphleteer at the accession of George III.[1] "Formed general oppositions," Lord Hardwicke told the Duke of Newcastle five years earlier, "are the most wicked combinations that men can enter into—worse and more corrupt than any administration that I ever yet saw."[2] At this time—already past the middle of the century—most politicians would still have professed to agree with both propositions, and vestiges of these attitudes continued to influence politics for the rest of the century. Persistent opposition to administration was considered immoral, especially by ministers themselves; and political parties, as they took

[1] [John Douglas], *Seasonable Hints from an Honest Man*, 1761.
[2] P. C. Yorke, *Life and Correspondence of Philip Yorke, Earl of Hardwicke*, Cambridge, 1913, III, 392.

shape from the 1760s, continued to be equated with the self-seeking factions of the earlier part of the century. Nevertheless, the two most significant developments of the century were the gradual acceptance of continuous "formed" opposition as a normal aspect of politics and of political parties as necessary associations of men proposing, and ready to carry out, changes of measures in alternative administrations.

These two developments were intimately connected. Men who were in fact opposing a ministry—as many of them always were, despite the opprobrium attached to opposition—had to develop justification for their conduct which distinguished it from "wicked" opposition. More important still, if they were to make any impression on the normal ministerial majorities, they had to organize their sympathizers in and out of Parliament, and create distinct identities for themselves as groups—that is, become parties with programs distinct from those of the ministry. The progress in these new directions, especially in the growth and acceptance of parties, was most marked after 1760, thanks to the reappearance of serious political and constitutional issues; but the grounds had been well laid in the first half of the century. Regular opposition was a political fact long before contemporaries ceased deploring it on every possible occasion, and with it were growing up "party" groupings larger than the personal connections of aristocrats and major politicians.

The Opposition

Any politician who persistently opposed every measure and every act of the king's ministers faced an uphill struggle. Arrayed against him were the prevailing views that "formed" opposition was factious and disloyal, that the king ought to have the ministers he wanted, and that every good subject ought to support them unless they were patently incompetent or wicked. In addition, he had to contend against the powerful ministerial machine of influence and patronage, with its hold over so many members, armed with nothing more than promises to use it better in the future or to dismantle it altogether. These disadvantages nevertheless did not prevent every important individual and group from opposing, often successfully, in just this way at some time during their careers. As a result they gradually made opposition respectable, even admirable, turning what they had once justified merely as a temporary expedient to save king and constitution from rapacious ministers into a normal convention of politics, providing an alternative ministry which represented a change of men *and* measures. The process was greatly helped by changes in the character of parliamentary opposition itself because of the growing importance of political and constitutional issues during the reign of George III.

In the age of Walpole and the Pelhams, the object of most politicians attacking the ministry was to drive a few men from office so that they could take their place while continuing to conduct the king's business in much the same way—only, so they promised, more honestly and efficiently. Almost equally acceptable to them was a private bargain with administration by which they would obtain places for themselves and become the colleagues of the very men they had previously condemned. Their opposition was, as contemporaries considered it, essentially factious—a personal quest for power and place with little concern for measures. They did not yet think of themselves while out of office as forming an alternative ministry committed to modifying, perhaps to reversing completely, the policies of the men they hoped to join or replace. By the last quarter of the century, however, they were coming to conceive of their purpose in exactly these terms. Opposition was ceasing to be a loose and temporary confederation of politicians without places and becoming a "party" with an organization, and even a program, of its own.

Before these changes took place—and they were never more than partially achieved by the Rockingham Whigs or by Fox's "party" after 1784—Opposition was a far less united coalition than was the ministry. Its size rose and fell on specific issues before the House during the course of a session and varied greatly from session to session of the same Parliament. The leading Opposition politicians could rarely estimate with any certainty the votes they might obtain against a government bill or in favor of their own motions and amendments. The discipline these leaders could exert over most of the members who normally voted with them—independent country gentlemen—was weaker than that which the most feeble ministry exerted over its supporters because these back-benchers distrusted the opposition politicians as thoroughly as they did those already in office.

The opposition of these independents was apolitical; it was directed at government as such, and the politicians who enjoyed their support while out of office would lose it as soon as they became ministers and betrayed their promises. The independents, despite their numbers in the House, therefore had little to do with the growth of Opposition "parties" and the new conception of Opposition as an alternative government because they remained outside the political connections. In other ways, though, the independents had a profound influence on the behavior and programs of these parties. Opposition oratory and promises were always tailored to their prejudices. Even in the reign of George III, when fewer of the independents consistently voted against every ministry, the patterns formed in the age of Walpole continued to affect the ideas of the political leaders. The economic reform proposals of the Rockingham party in the 1780s were refinements of the place bills of Sir Robert's opponents, and the early propaganda for parliamentary reform in the 1770s and 1780s was filled with quotations from the pamphlets and speeches of these same men denouncing the corruption of the political system. Winning the support of the independents remained a constant and necessary goal of every opposition.

At the same time, the reliance of the opposition politicians on the intransigent antiadministration independents always weakened these politicians with the political establishment during the first half of the century. Most of the country gentlemen were "Tories" to contemporaries and in their own estimation, a few of them were active Jacobites, and a good many more harbored Jacobite sympathies—that is, they were men or the descendants and associates of men who had supported the Oxford-Bolingbroke ministry—and because a few of them continued to dabble in "treason," all of them were suspected of working for the return of the Stuarts. Those who were not Tories were apt to be "real Whigs" looking back to the ideals of the seventeenth-century radicals and suspected of "republicanism" and other dangerous designs on things as they had come to be. For a professed Whig—as all the important Opposition leaders except Bolingbroke and Sir William Wyndham were—to seek such allies raised questions of his own loyalty to the dynasty without gaining him any real favor with his new friends, who rightly suspected his motives and sincerity in promising to adopt and act on their principles. The ministers could always play on this fundamental distrust between the opposition back-benchers and the politicians, counteracting the appeal of platitudes about honest, patriotic, and cheap administration. Nevertheless, ministers never succeeded in completely discrediting their critics, and eventually every administration was driven to come to terms with the more important ones.

Unity among the active politicians out of place was fully as hard to achieve as was real cooperation between the independents and the politicians. All too often in the first half of the century, the politicians acted as so many detached individuals or small groups of friends and relatives, almost hopelessly divided by mutual jealousies and rivalries for place. "Lord Carteret and Lord Bolingbroke had no correspondence at all," Lord Hervey wrote of Walpole's opponents; "Mr. Pulteney and Lord Bolingbroke hated one another; Lord Carteret and Pulteney were jealous of one another; Sir William Wyndham and Pulteney the same; whilst Lord Chesterfield had a little correspondence with them all, but was confided in by none of them."[3] Chesterfield himself expected this opposition, on the very eve of its triumph over Walpole, to be

> neither . . . united nor well conducted. Those who should lead it will make it their business to break and divide it; and they will succeed; I mean Carteret and Pulteney. Their behavior for these few years has, in my mind, plainly shown their views and their negotiations with the Court. . . . [They] . . . desire to get in with a few, by negotiation, and not by victory with numbers, who they fear, might presume upon their strength, and grow troublesome to their generals.[4]

[3] John, Lord Hervey, *Some Materials towards Memoirs of the Reign of George II*, ed. R. Sedgwick, London, 1931, I, 256.
[4] Philip Dormer Stanhope, fourth earl of Chesterfield, *Letters*, ed. B. Dobrée [London], 1932, II, 467–468.

In this situation, ministers could often reduce professed unions among their opponents to mutual recrimination by negotiating with a few individuals or groups among them. As a result much of the history of opposition is the story of repeated but only occasionally successful attempts to forge some common bond of unity among the politicians out of place that was strong enough not only to unite them against ministerial bland-ishments for the moment, but also to keep them together subse-quently as ministers, once they had been successful in destroying an administration. Perceptible progress in this direction became apparent only when the differences between men in and out of office began to turn on issues as well as the possession of places.

Between the Hanoverian succession and the accession of George III, the ministers and their critics rarely differed seri-ously on domestic affairs. Party loyalties—in the sense of parties representing divergent philosophies of government—influenced their rivalries even less; although "party"—as contemporaries often used the word to mean a group of politicians allied in the pursuit or retention of office—played a conspicuous role. The few real differences among them concerned foreign policy, and even these were usually artificially cultivated. In the reigns of William and Anne, indeed, the lines between the "Ins" and the "Outs" had been drawn in terms of party and ideological dif-ferences, and immediately after 1714 it looked as though the pattern of Anne's reign would continue—that the government and its opponents at any time, despite many individual excep-tions, could be described as broadly "Whig" or "Tory" in tone. But the Whig victory turned into such a total rout of all pro-fessed Tories (not only were they purged from Administration, but they were also outnumbered by more than two to one in every Parliament after 1715) that the new masters could soon safely fall out among themselves, which they continued to do for the rest of the century. Important parliamentary conflicts after 1714 were always between Whigs and Whigs, never between Whigs and Tories.

The leading Opposition orators under George I and George II were, almost without exception, either one-time administration supporters who had quarreled with the current ministers or professed Whigs concerned with making such a nuisance of themselves that the ministers would buy them off. Their most active and dependable followers were, as usual in contemporary politics, their relatives and personal connections. Another group of votes on which they could depend belonged to the friends and dependents of the Prince of Wales whenever their was an heir of age.

"I always hated the rascal, but now I hate him worse than ever," George II shouted to Lord Hervey about his son Frederick, Prince of Wales. "No, no! he shall not come and act any of his silly plays here, false, lying, cowardly, nauseous, puppy."[5] The loathing that the Hanoverian kings and their successors felt for each other meant that the Prince of Wales and his entourage almost always opposed the king and his ministers. Whoever was in favor at court was anathema at Leicester House (the residence of the prince, and hence the name "Leicester House Faction" for his friends); and whoever was "well" with the prince could be assumed an opponent of the ministry. Every politician out of office made his court to the prince—Sir Robert Walpole in 1717, all of Walpole's enemies at different times between 1722 and 1742, Pitt and the Bedfords in the late 1740s and 1750s, and all of the Foxities after the early 1780s, when there was again a mature Prince of Wales, as there had not been during the first two decades of George III's reign.

This persistent animosity between the king and prince helped to make Opposition respectable by showing it to be unquestioningly loyal to the dynasty. The politician who was advising the successor to the throne could hardly be accused of flirting with Jacobitism. Unfortunately, the intensity of hatred that George I and II felt for their eldest sons also meant that any politician who was active in the prince's service became personally obnoxious to the king, as unacceptable to him as a candidate for place as was the man who criticized Hanover. The elder Pitt enraged George II on both counts, and the king had to be

[5] John, Lord Hervey, *Some Materials towards Memoirs of the Reign of George II,* ed. R. Sedgwick, London, 1931, III, 885.

coerced by threats of resignation from the other ministers in the Pelhams' administration to consent to his appointment to a minor place in 1746. George III did not feel quite as violently toward his eldest son, but his personal animus toward Fox and his friends was intensified by the belief that they had corrupted the prince's morals.

Besides the prince's passing attraction for active politicians during what they hoped would be only a temporary exclusion from office under his father, his small court always provided the nucleus for men gambling on futures in the succeeding reign, and who were willing to wait for their rewards until their master became king. The truly competent men were never this patient under the first two Georges. Walpole used a temporary reconciliation that he had negotiated between the prince and George I to reenter the ministry in 1720; the elder Pitt deserted Leicester House in 1746 and again in 1757. Even the merely ambitious were not always steadily loyal; George Bubb Dodington became notorious for the number of times he abandoned Frederick to join the ministry and then quitted administration to return to the prince. The political friends of the prince after 1784 were forced to be more consistent in their attachment. The Foxites were so much aware that their only hope of office would come at the prince's accession that they reversed their long-professed principles of limiting the freedom of the crown and demanded an unrestricted regency for the prince when George III went temporarily insane in 1788, so that he could bring them to office.

The Leicester House regulars in the first half of the century were all second-rate, and failed completely when they finally obtained power. Sir Spencer Compton, George II's favorite when he was Prince of Wales, was so absurd as to ask Walpole, whom he was to succeed as First Lord of the Treasury, to write the new king's first address to Parliament. He immediately passed into the decent obscurity of a peerage and the Lord Presidency of the Council, although Walpole allowed him an unregarded voice in the inner councils of his ministry. Lord Bute, George III's Spencer Compton, indeed played a more decisive political part for three years, although he played it in a manner that destroyed any chance of permanent success for any minor changes in the methods of government which he and the king may have intended. He was finally excluded from the king's person and eventually hounded into virtual exile abroad. The Leicester House "party" by itself, far from offering an alternative ministry, rarely offered even a competent minor minister.

Nevertheless, because many of its members sat in Parliament, and because the prince in his capacity as duke of Cornwall had extensive electoral influence in the Cornish boroughs, the faction always provided a numerically important group of opposition votes. When a ministry was tottering for other reasons, Leicester House could hasten its defeat. Sir Robert Walpole's loss of the House of Commons in 1742 owed much to the fact that Frederick (who hated him) had turned the Cornish boroughs against the government. This, combined with the temporary loss of the normally "safe" Scottish seats, reduced his majority to such insignificance that other time-serving members deserted him, and Walpole's measures began to be defeated. On the other hand, the few occasions when the prince and his father were on good terms (or when there was no prince of age) favored the ministry—sometimes because of the additional votes at their disposal, but more often because the prince no longer provided a focus for other opposition groups. Walpole was aided in weathering the excise crisis in Parliament and in winning the subsequent general election because the prince was supporting the ministry at the moment. The Pelhams were aided in maintaining control of the ministry after 1742 because Frederick sided with them for a time after Walpole's fall. And the all-inclusive character of Henry Pelham's administration after 1751 owed a great deal to the death of Prince Frederick. Because there was no prince to provide this focus for Opposition in the 1760s, the personal and ideological differences of competing factions and individuals ran rampant.

Although the politicians would probably never have been able to unite under any circumstances, the absence of one acknowledged leader standing above them made it impossible. The king's uncle, the duke of Cumberland, aspired to the role, but he was too closely tied to the Newcastle-Rockinghams, and in any event he died in the autumn of 1765. By the time there was again a prince of age, around 1780, conditions had sufficiently changed to make him less politically important personally; George IV as prince was only the ally of opposition politicians now closely bound together by common loyalties and ideas. The Prince of Wales, like his father the king, found himself being pushed out of his old influence in politics by the end of the century.

No combination of opposition connections with the Leicester House faction alone was strong enough to disrupt a ministry, even with the votes of the hard core of Tories and anti-administration independents. To succeed in bringing down the administration, or even in forcing it to come to an accommodation with some of them, the opposition politicians also had to win the support of many of those independents who ordinarily gave silent votes to the ministry out of a sense of duty to support the king's government, whether they felt any enthusiasm for it or not. Thus the politicians had to play steadily to the prejudices and inconsistent political notions of these independents. And because these members might be swayed by movements of "public opinion," they also had to appeal beyond them to the views of the mass of country gentlemen and merchants—the only groups outside Parliament with much perceptible influence on politics for most of the century. These men, although passive in the continuous struggle for power and place among the politicians, were always potential allies for any opposition. Most of them held the same antiadministration prejudices that the more intransigent back-benchers, "Whig" or "Tory," made their way of life. If they could once be persuaded that a ministry was more than normally corrupt, or that it was actively threatening their material interests or their "liberties," they could be roused to active protest. If the outcry became loud or widespread enough, the ministry would be more influenced than by the best organized opposition campaign within Parliament itself. Not only would proadministration independents begin to withhold their votes—which could be very serious if enough of them did so—but ministers, courtiers, even occasionally the king himself, would also begin to think in terms of an accommodation with the opposition politicians to quiet the discontent and ensure their own political futures. Thus the opposition politicians always devoted much energy to organizing and manipulating the large reservoir of potentially favorable "public opinion" inside and outside Parliament.

In the process of courting independents and cultivating antiadministration prejudices outside Parliament, the politicians developed a remarkably consistent program. The same ideas, many of them borrowed from the radical Whig literature of the late seventeenth century, appear in the oratory of all Opposition debaters, in the rhetoric of their pamphlets and newspapers, and in all opposition bills and amendments throughout the century. Opposition politicians always began by representing themselves as the true "patriots," determined to rescue the king from the thrall of designing ministers and to restore the balance of the constitution which these men were trying to overset for their own personal advantage. Sir Robert Walpole, during his brief period in Opposition, set the tone that all subsequent orators imitated when he charged that Sunderland and Stanhope were "running the nation into an aristocracy . . . so as to establish themselves and be able for the future to give laws to the King and his son and even remove them when they shall think proper."[6] His imitators talked of restoring the independence of Parliament, curbing an overgrown executive, and rooting out "corruption" everywhere (by which they meant all ministerial and crown influence.) Since the country gentlemen, freeholders, merchants, and tradesmen distrusted the executive and would believe most stories of scandals—political and financial—at court and among the ministerial supporters in Parliament, all oppositions made sweeping accusations of personal corruption and charges of undue influence by the crown and its ministers in Parliament, in hopes that some of them would turn a vote or two on the back-benches. They proposed to effect a cure for all this corruption they had ferreted out by introducing place bills.

[6] Quoted in *Letters from George III to Lord Bute 1756–1766,* ed. R. Sedgwick, London, 1936, p. xvii.

These bills were normally of an impracticably sweeping character in the first half of the century, encompassing every place of profit under the crown. As a result they were defeated on the spot, amended out of recognition, or thrown out in the House of Lords. Their sponsors did not believe in them, even in principle, and dropped any such ideas of reform when they obtained office themselves, just as they did their still more "radical" promises to repeal the Septennial Act of 1716 (extending the life of Parliament from three years to seven years) in favor of shorter Parliaments, to restore the Privy Council to the place usurped by the cabinet, to cut back the army, and to curb the King's Civil List. Nevertheless, the later eighteenth-century oppositions by no means abandoned this mode of appeal to back-benchers and opinion outside Parliament. Instead the leaders came to believe in their own professed remedies. The Rockingham Whigs turned the place-bill program into a serious possibility by proposing to eliminate only the more obvious means for influencing members of Parliament; they made enactment of their proposals a condition for accepting office in April 1782 and carried them into law during the next few months. In this revised form, a standard plank of the old opposition platform initiated the process of administrative reform and played a part in destroying the old methods of political management in the following decades.

Opposition orators also regularly tried to turn the economic interest groups against the administration. To arouse the body of merchants, always distrustful of the government, they posed as the defenders of the interests of English trade, while representing ministers as the pawns of France or Spain, selling out vital English concerns and negligent of commerce in every particular. This line of attack was particularly prominent in the opposition to Walpole, to all the ministries containing men responsible for the Peace of Paris in 1763, and to those ministries that tried to tax the American colonies. Opposition speakers also played up ministerial "deals" with the moneyed interests and great trading companies to encourage the average merchant's antagonism toward the economic oligarchs—a common tactic pioneered by the Tory orators of the reigns of William and Anne toward the Whig Bank of England, which was always revived whenever large loans were to be negotiated or the East India Company's charter revised or renewed. At other times, inconsistently, Opposition politicians would attempt to persuade the country gentlemen that mercantile interests dominated the ministry, forcing the landowners to foot the tax bill for adventures that would profit merchants alone. This argument always became popular toward the end of every war. George III and Lord Bute, both of whom naively thought in Opposition clichés, believed it and acted on it in 1760–1762 in their precipitate attempts to end the war and to get rid of Pitt and Newcastle. There were, however, definite if unspoken limits to Opposition exploitation of real economic grievances, ready as its members were to make the most of imaginary ones. No politician in Parliament ever espoused the cause of the "lower orders" in England, nor, until the age of the French Revolution, did any of the more radical politicians and propagandists out of Parliament; those who did so then were regarded with horror by the majority of their fellow reformers. The laboring poor were to suffer in deferential silence, leaving politics to the governing classes and middling sort.

Opposition politicians of course seized on every ministerial proposal or blunder that could be twisted to indicate arbitrary designs on the part of kings and ministers or covert attacks on English "liberties." The reasonable Excise Bill of 1733, proposing an excise tax on wine and tobacco to prevent smuggling and improve government income while lowering direct taxes, was represented as a project to terrorize the subject into paying unlimited financial exactions at the whim of the minister by introducing government spies into every household. The Grenville ministry's petulant attack on Wilkes in 1763 by a general warrant, although intended only to destroy one obnoxious individual, was turned into a ministerial project to revive the powers of arbitrary search and arrest and to invade the liberties of members of Parliament. Wilkes's repeated expulsions from the House after his three elections in 1769–1770 and the seating of his defeated opponent were construed as designs to turn an already subservient Parliament into a co-optive body of ministerialists, totally independent of its constituents. When the younger Pitt remained in office during the winter of 1784, despite repeated defeats in the House of Commons, and then appealed successfully to the electorate, he and the king were charged with plotting to destroy Parliament and substitute occasional appeals to the "people" in its place. When Pitt proposed that the regency to be offered to the Prince of Wales in 1789 be severely limited because the king was likely to recover, Burke even went so far as to accuse him of intending to seize the throne himself.

The opposition did not leave their accusations to recommend themselves to the political classes by self-evident truth alone. They subsidized newspapers and political pamphlets with more success than administration; the best papers were usually in their pay and most of the famous pamphlets were written for their causes. Still more important in their scheme for achieving their aims was the organization of petitioning campaigns, addresses to the king, and concerted resolutions by county meetings and grand juries to enforce their claim that their ideas represented the true opinion of honest Englishmen. In the first half of the century, petitions had been used with considerable skill and success to buttress the attacks on the Excise Bill, the demand for the war with Spain, and the repeal of the Jewish Naturalization Bill. But these campaigns had been limited in scope. Only selected places (usually London and the more populous boroughs) and economic groups whose interests could be represented as directly threatened by the government's actions had been inspired to petition. During the reign of George III, these petitioning campaigns became much more extensive and better organized: a growing political consciousness everywhere in the country was encouraging its further development. In turn, the petitioning movements assisted the growth of extraparliamentary pressure groups, which by threatening to escape the control of the politicians, introduced a new force into later eighteenth-century politics.

The Rockingham Whigs were the chief architects of the expanded use of petitioning, having first tried the method when in office in 1765–1766 to create sufficient pressure from the mercantile interests all over England to force George III and Parliament to accept the repeal of the Stamp Act. This program worked so well that the Rockingham Whigs decided to use it to harness the general ferment caused by the Wilkesite troubles in 1769–1770 to a petitioning campaign in favor of a change of ministers and a new Parliament. But already more radical politicians outside Parliament, especially in London, were learning the potentialities of the new techniques. To these men, nourished by a submerged stream of political radicalism flowing from the Civil Wars and the earliest days of Whiggism, Opposition was as tainted as the ministry: the parliamentary rivalries were only so many insignificant squabbles among members of the same exclusive club. The Rockinghams found it impossible, even with the cooperation of other opposition groups, to limit the petitions they organized all over England to the narrow aims of their own parliamentary projects. Instead, the objectives formulated by Wilkes's London supporters, the Society for the Bill of Rights—short Parliaments, instructions to members, franchise reform—found places in some of the petitions. If the radicals had not fallen out among themselves, parliamentary reform might have become a serious issue a decade earlier than it did. Opinion out of doors, invited repeatedly to express itself against the ministry and the majority of the House of Commons, was already beginning to speak against the political structure itself and to show itself less subservient to direction from above than it had formerly been.

Nevertheless, Opposition politicians continued to inspire petitions themselves and to exploit, if they possibly could, any others for which they were not directly responsible. Their repeated attempts to start general petitioning campaigns against American policy and the American war, however, never succeeded during the early and mid-1770s. The idea of making the colonists pay for their defense and then punishing them for their insubordination was too popular with most Englishmen for opposition arguments of the folly and futility of that course of action to make much of an impression. Furthermore the growing divisions between the conservative politicians—who only wanted to change men and measures—and the radicals—who wished to change the whole system of government—now turned the wording of every petition into a battleground. Despite these failures and the mounting evidence that petitioning was potentially dangerous to the Establishment, whether in office or in Opposition, the politicians returned to this device as soon as opinion began to move against the ministry and the war in 1779. They were already in the midst of planning a massive program of petitions against increasing royal influence and financial extravagance when they were faced by an even more widespread agitation organized independently of them by the Rev. Christopher Wyville and his associates—the Yorkshire or Associated Counties Movement of 1780. The demands of these men—which they planned to enforce through coordinated petitions from all over England—initially paralleled those of the parliamentary politicians, but they soon extended far beyond them to include substantial parliamentary reform. (See pages 144–145.) The politicians struggled in vain to contain the movement. Although they usually succeeded in moderating the more violent wordings proposed for the petitions, and most of them refused to cooperate with the national organization the reformers created to back up the petitions, they never really got the movement under control.

The increasingly radical demands of the reformers, whether or not formally inserted in the petitions as presented to Parliament, undercut the parliamentary campaign to curb crown influence in Parliament, because the back-benchers were more frightened by popular agitation threatening radical changes in familiar institutions than they were disgusted by the misconduct of the war and ever-higher taxes. Their fears were intensified by the results of another simultaneous but unconnected petitioning movement involving still lower social groups—the Gordon Riots of June 1780—when the London mob rose after the presentation of a petition (which thousands of them and their equivalents elsewhere in England had signed) demanding the repeal of some minor concessions granted to Roman Catholics two years earlier. For several days the mob burned and pillaged the City and West End unopposed. (See page 146.)

The violent reaction among the political classes to threatened anarchy temporarily discredited mass petitioning and extraparliamentary associations as tools to be used by respectable politicians to organize opinion against the ministry, but they became more popular than ever with the growing number of new groups and interests now determined to take part in national affairs. The opposition groups, by introducing organized public opinion into politics and by demonstrating the methods by which it could bring pressure to bear upon the government, were also making themselves susceptible to the same pressure. As they came to rely on outside opinion as well as on parliamentary maneuvre and backstairs intrigue in their search for office, they were forced to adopt consistent programs more in accord with what the articulate public wanted and to make some show of implementing them if they did gain office. When they succeeded, as they did in 1782, they could force themselves on the king and accomplish some of their aims. If they failed to heed public opinion, as they did in the Fox-North coalition (see pages 151–156) and again during the regency crisis of 1788, the reaction against them out of doors now powerfully reinforced the remaining influence of the crown and administration in discrediting them. The rout of the Foxites in 1784 was far more complete than was foreseen by the ministerialists, thanks to a generally prevailing feeling that Fox and his friends had betrayed their principles in a manner too reminiscent of the older politics. The Foxites also suffered at the general election of 1790 after a similar public abandonment of principle over the regency. Public opinion was thus playing a considerable role in turning the older self-seeking opposition factions into parties representing possible alternative governments.

The Development of Parties Before 1780

Political parties by the 1790s differed as much from the parties of Anne's reign or the factions during Walpole's and Newcastle's heyday as they did from the Liberal and Conservative parties of the late nineteenth century. Because party was in a state of growth and transformation throughout the century, it is impossible to fix any sort of pattern that describes all periods. Attitudes once thought typically Whig came to make their advocates seem typically Tory. Party labels, which had reflected real differences of opinion among the politically influential during the reigns of William and Anne, lost their ideological basis. The old Tory groups effectively disappeared from the national scene after 1714, even though around 150 members described as Tories sat in subsequent Parliaments. Various Whig factions, divided only by personal rivalries, vied for control of the administration. Then, during the 1760s and early 1770s new national and international problems introduced more serious divisions, so that a change of ministers began to represent a change of policy. At the same time that the parties were beginning again to represent real divisions of opinion among Englishmen, they were becoming more responsible to opinion outside the narrow parliamentary class, more aware of its importance, and more anxious to exploit it. Politics became increasingly concerned with issues and programs, although the earlier personal, factional rivalry for power and place as ends in themselves had by no means disappeared.

The eighteenth-century parties originated during the Restoration. The Cavalier Parliament, after its first paroxysm of loyalty was spent, began to divide along the lines of "Court" and "Country," attitudes of mind which continued for the next century. The typical Country member was an independent country gentleman, suspicious of courtiers and politicians, and (before 1688) increasingly alarmed by the royal drift toward Catholicism and a French alliance, which raised the spectre of absolutism. He favored limitations on the powers of the crown and ministers and wished to increase the independence and authority of Parliament. Politicians out of favor adopted the sentiments of these men, occasionally out of conviction but more often to gain their votes in Parliament. The Court member was a man in office or in some other way connected with the government or hopeful of getting something out of it, so that politicians who had once acted as spokesmen for Country views were easily transformed into Court apologists once they received office. The lines of Court and Country thus cut across the later divisions of Whig and Tory. Both these groups had Court and Country wings, usually differing more from each other in their attitude toward any ministry than Court Whigs differed from Court Tories or Country Whigs from Country Tories. Because of this similarity of Court and Country views, regardless of other labels men adopted, the two great "parties" appeared to reverse their philosophies completely in the early decades of the century, when the Whigs became permanently "In" and the Tories, "Out."

In the later seventeenth century, and even through the reign of Anne, Country sentiments and Whiggism were closely connected, although never identical. But as the Whigs began to taste the pleasures of office under William and during the middle years of Anne, antiexecutive prejudices, which had been so general before the Revolution, waned. After the Whig triumph of 1714 they disappeared entirely except among a group of purists—the "Real Whigs," as they called themselves, the spiritual ancestors of many of the later radicals. At the same time the Tories, originally courtiers or at least believers in divine right and nonresistance, men who exalted the power of the crown, began losing their zeal for monarchy and ministers. When they were permanently excluded from office after 1714, they were converted into opponents of all administrations so rapidly that "Tory" became increasingly a synonym for independent, antiadministration country gentlemen.

The famous labels "Whig" and "Tory" had come into existence during the Exclusionist controversy of 1679–1681. This crisis took the form of an assault by the organized Country party, created by the earl of Shaftesbury, on the Court party, built up by the earl of Danby to marshal the votes of all members of Parliament indebted in some way to the crown. Danby's organization was the first thoroughgoing attempt to create and maintain a body of supporters in Parliament through the use of influence, patronage, and in some cases more blatant bribery than later opinion would have tolerated. When Danby's Court party disintegrated in the hysteria engendered by the Popish Plot of 1679, many royalists temporarily joined Shaftesbury's ranks, and for a time he seemed likely to carry all before him. The lines between the two sides were most clearly drawn, however, not over the Exclusion Bills themselves, but between those men who signed petitions during 1680 demanding the meeting of the prorogued Parliament and those who signed loyal addresses "abhorring" this "unconstitutional" pressure on the king. The party labels during these few months, "Petitioners" and "Abhorrers," were rapidly superseded by the derogatory epithets, "Whig" and "Tory," exchanged by the contending factions in this first and most violent party clash. When an Abhorrer called a Petitioner a Whig he intended to suggest an unflattering similarity between him and the covenanted Scotsmen who had recently been murdering bishops on Scottish moors. The Petitioner, however, proudly adopted the name to indicate his preference for parliamentary supremacy, a strictly limited monarchy, and toleration for Protestant Dissenters. Similarly Abhorrers forgot that Tories were Irish Catholic bandits who murdered Protestants in Irish bogs and accepted the Whig slur of Tory to indicate their more exalted view of the place of the crown in politics, their unquestioning loyalty to the person of the king, and their belief in the supremacy of the Established Church.

Within these general positions, the labels Whig and Tory rapidly came to cover a broad spectrum of opinion. At their most radical, Whigs shaded off into doctrinaire republicans; Tories, after 1688, at their most reactionary, became Jacobites. In the middle, the two groups overlapped in many men who, if pressed on a crucial constitutional or religious issue, might take on a clearly Whig or Tory stance, but who were in no sense rigid in their views. These men often cooperated to hold the balance between the more extreme partisans of both their parties, because they found it easier to work with moderates of the opposite complexion than they did with the rabid exponents of their own general beliefs. Marlborough and Godolphin, court Tories, found it essential to get rid of the Rochester and Nottingham Tories and to work more closely with the Whig Junto — so closely, in fact, that they came to seem more Whig than Tory to their contemporaries, and they suffered accordingly when the doctrinaire Tories achieved power under Harley and Bolingbroke in 1710.

Despite ambiguities in the exact meaning of the party

labels as applied to individuals, it is still possible to speak meaningfully of the existence of Whigs and Tories as an essential part of the political structure of England from the 1680s through 1714. This does not mean, of course, that the politics of the era took the form of a simple duel between two clearly defined parties comprehending the majority of men in Parliament. Both parties were loose confederations of factions, each centered on some individual or group with more or less distinct Whig or Tory views. Neither party had a comprehensive organization, and at no time did the factions that composed them ever include all men in politics—probably not even a majority of them. Nor did any administration, whether labeled Whig or Tory, ever include representatives of all the Whig or Tory factions. Nevertheless, administrations composed primarily of Tory factions differed in their policies from ones composed primarily of Whig groups, and major reconstructions of the ministry in which numerous individuals and groups of one hue were replaced by those of the other *did* signify changes in policy. In 1710 the change in ministry resulted in the complete reversal of the war and foreign policy of the previous government, and the ensuing domestic policies of the Harley-Bolingbroke ministry, especially toward Dissenters, were quite opposite from those pursued by Godolphin, Marlborough, and the Whig Junto. Alternations between Whig and Tory represented new measures fully as much as they did new ministers. The same was true of changes in the complexion of Parliament at the triennial elections. A House of Commons in which Tory partisans predominated would not pass what contemporaries recognized as Whiggish bills, and vice versa; the House of Lords, where the Whigs had obtained a permanent majority, had to be packed by a mass creation of Tory peers in order to approve the Tory preliminaries of the Peace of Utrecht. The politics of the age become incomprehensible if the very real and serious party rivalries over policy, greater than any factional ambitions for place, are ignored.

The situation changed between the Hanoverian succession and the French Revolution. Although the names of Whig and Tory continued to be used, any attempt to explain the politics of the period in those terms introduces confusion as serious as does the attempt to explain politics before 1714 without them. Whig politicians turned the Hanoverian succession into a party victory and destroyed the Tory party as it had existed in national politics during the last years of Anne's reign. The Tory ministers and all their adherents were expelled from office, and a Tory ancestry or affiliation remained an excuse for continued exclusion for many decades—even though individual "Tory" families were allowed to make their peace with ministers and become prominent "Whigs," as the Foxes, Legges, Winningtons, and Gowers all did under Walpole and the Pelhams. A surviving "Toryism," occasionally pro-Jacobite but more commonly in the form of simple antiadministration independence, also remained widespread among the political classes outside the ruling oligarchy. Even during the "Whig" heyday, from 1714 to 1760, the majority of Englishmen were more Tory than Whig in this sense. But the minority were in complete control of the administration and in effective control of Parliament, so that the political conflicts at the national level were between various Whig factions and individuals, not between Whigs and Tories.

The result was that parties ceased to exist in the sense that they had existed before 1714. No real differences over policy divided the ministry from its active opponents, while Opposition was too discordant a confederation of mutually jealous displaced Whig politicians, old Tories, and apolitical independents to achieve more than a temporary unity over a particular motion or for the course of a single session. The closest thing to a party, even in its limited later eighteenth-century sense, could be found in the heart of administration itself—the "Old Corps" of Walpoleans, forged by Sir Robert and the duke of Newcastle (who perfected the methods of influence pioneered by the earl of Danby) out of their personal connections, those of their closest personal and political allies, and miscellaneous place-holders. This group, which numbered around one hundred and fifty members, had sufficient coherence (thanks to the spoils of power) to survive the fall of Walpole. It formed the basis of every stable administration until the accession of George III, and provided the core of the later Rockingham Whigs, the group that would eventually contribute the most to the creation of "party" in a more modern sense. The leaders of the "Old Corps" naturally tried to appropriate the label of "Whig" exclusively to themselves, but there was no disguising the fact that their important rivals, once their colleagues, were as Whiggish as they themselves.

Walpole himself established the pattern of Whig opposition in 1717 when he and Townshend broke with Sunderland and Stanhope, ostensibly because of disagreements over foreign policy, but actually because of clashing ambitions for control of the ministry. The causes of the rupture in the ministry, the conduct of the ex-ministers while out of office, and the manner in which their opposition ended were often repeated in politics until the 1760s. Walpole and Townshend took with them their own immediate connections, then allied with some other small groups of discontented Whigs already clustered around the Prince of Wales (as usual at odds with his father), and assiduously cultivated the remaining Tories and independents, the largest group of steady antiadministration votes. This combination was strong and effective enough to embarrass the ministry seriously, which was all that Walpole and his friends wished. They had no use for the old Tories and little more for the other Whigs, so they contrived their peace with their old rivals by reconciling the prince with his father and obtained office for themselves and their circle, while leaving the rest of their temporary allies, Whig and Tory, in the wilderness. They made no significant terms about policy, and entertained no thoughts of totally reconstructing the ministry on the basis of a new alliance of politicians formed out of office.

The history of the oppositions to Sir Robert between 1720 and 1742 and to his immediate successors is the reenactment of his own brief opposition over a much longer period. As he and Townshend went into opposition because they felt themselves undercut within the ministry, so most of Sir Robert's enemies drifted or were pushed out of office because of power struggles within the administration and at court. Some prominent members of his early ministry, most notably Lords Carteret and Chesterfield, had originally been attached to Sunderland and

Stanhope, and insisted on remaining independent of Walpole. Others more closely connected with Sir Robert, including William Pulteney and eventually Lord Townshend himself, began to chafe because the "Great Man" refused them the power to which they felt they were entitled. Rather than conciliate any of these potential rivals, Walpole ejected them. His rigorous disciplining of defectors during the exicse crisis of 1733, when many influential men were dismissed, increased still further the numbers and the ability of Opposition, especially Lord Cobham and his "Cubs"—Pitt, the Grenvilles, and George Lyttelton. Renewed quarrels within the royal family turned the Prince of Wales and his followers permanently against the minister. But the growing number of "Outs" never coalesced into a single group (or even a series of largish groups) with programs significantly different from those being followed by the ministry, or with an internal unity strong enough to force even a partial reconstruction of the ministry, to say nothing of being able to offer themselves as a complete alternative administration. Instead of becoming a party or a set of parties as the "Outs" after 1760 did, they remained a loose confederation of factions and detached individuals, united in their desire to get Walpole out of office, but beyond that hopelessly divided by their own competing ambitions for places. So even though they eventually accomplished their one common aim of forcing Walpole to resign, they could easily be neutralized and then pulverized by gradual absorption into the "Old Corps" by Walpole's own lieutenants.

In 1742 a few of the most prominent critics—among them Carteret and Pulteney—were immediately placed ostentatiously in impotent places in the administration still controlled by the Pelhams, and others were put off with vague promises of new arrangements later, thus driving further wedges between the already divided "Outs." The maneuver worked so well that when, four years later, the king tried to get rid of the Pelhams altogether, his nominees, the same Carteret and Pulteney, were unable to form a ministry at all. No one would serve under them, and the king was forced to settle for the Pelhams. They then proceeded to disintegrate the remaining opposition by detaching from it, piecemeal, every individual and group of importance and incorporating them in their own administration. By the end of the 1740s Opposition, far from being a powerful rival of and potential substitute for the ministry, was politically insignificant. The last chance it had of reemerging as a potential party disappeared with the death of the Prince of Wales in 1751.

When significant opposition groups reappeared briefly in the three years following Henry Pelham's death in 1754, they differed somewhat in character and composition from the factions that had existed between Walpole's consolidation of power and the creation of the Pelhamite coalition. They represent a transitional stage between these groups and the "parties" that took shape in the 1760s and which they prefigure in some ways. Instead of being formed by the gradual confederation of detached individuals and groups that had drifted into opposition against a securely established ministry, they arose out of the total collapse of the previous coalition in a three way struggle for power among Newcastle, Henry Fox, and the elder Pitt for the succession to Henry Pelham's commanding position. Nearly all the active politicians polarized around one of these leaders, creating three large parties that for three years entered and left administration as blocs; instability persisted as long as attempts were made to create ministries out of only one or two of the contending groups. Although they had originated in nothing more than the old contest for power and place, they became increasingly involved in questions of diplomatic and military policy in the opening stages of the war with France; and it was the threat of national disaster in 1757 which finally brought them together again in a coalition even more comprehensive than that engineered by Henry Pelham in the late 1740s. Newcastle agreed to leave the war to Pitt; Pitt willingly left parliamentary management and patronage to Newcastle; and Fox gave up his political pretensions for the extremely lucrative pay-office and the opportunity to make an enormous fortune.

In these conflicts of the 1740s and 1750s the old labels of Whig and Tory meant nothing, as contempories realized clearly enough, even though they still tried to use them with emotive significance. "Does any candid and intelligent man seriously believe, that at this time of day," asked a pamphleteer in 1761, "there subsists any party distinction amongst us, that is not merely nominal?"[7] Everyone in politics was some sort of Whig, in that he now unhesitatingly accepted not only the principles of the Revolution Settlement (all save the Jacobites had done that since 1688), but also the conventions of political management which the "professional" Whigs had worked out during the first half of the century. The politicians knew that the conflicts that began with the accession of George III had nothing to do with the old platitudes of Whig and Tory; indeed, they rarely used the labels any more in their private correspondence or parliamentary debate, although they continued to employ them loosely in pamphlets and propaganda intended for the uninitiated. Rather the divisions now revolved around new issues which changed the content and some of the characteristics of politics.

Issues were nothing new in English politics. In the years between the Revolution and the Hanoverian succession, they determined the party divisions between Whig and Tory. Despite much familiar jockeying for power and place, politics ultimately revolved around the preservation of the Protestant succession and the Revolution Settlement, the place of religious Dissenters in English life, and (less overtly expressed) the continued political predominance of the landed classes. These issues were not, in fact, definitely settled by the peaceful Hanoverian succession in 1714. They remained in the background, with a Stuart restoration through foreign arms an ingredient in the maneuvering of the Tory minority in Parliament and occasionally flirted with by some Opposition Whigs, until the disastrous failure of the Jacobite rising of 1745 demonstrated that all important Englishmen, however unenthusiastic about the Hanoverians and their ministers, acquiesced in the new order worked out since 1688. Between 1745 and the mid-1760s there were few vital domestic problems to plague the politicians and to pose ques-

[7] [John Douglas], *Seasonable Hints from an Honest Man,* quoted in *English Historical Documents,* vol. 10, 1714–1783, ed. D. B. Horn and M. Ransome, New York, 1957, pp. 203–204.

tions about the future course of English institutions. From the mid-1760s onward, however, a series of interrelated issues arose concerning the central institutions of English politics and the whole structure of imperial relations. In one area after another everything that had seemed securely established by the 1750s began to tremble, until finally the entire order seemed to face a fundamental challenge in the ideas of the French Revolution.

The trouble began with quarrels between George III and the politicians, and among the politicians themselves, over the proper relations between king, ministers, and Parliament. In origin, the arguments put forward by the Whig oligarchy were little more than the outraged attempts of displaced politicians to blacken their rivals and to justify their own claims to office on high constitutional principles contrived for the occasion. But the issues thus raised quickly became more than propaganda. The opposition spokesmen came to believe them themselves and proved powerful and effective enough to create the impression outside Parliament that the king intended to violate the constitution, and, through undue use of the influence of the crown, might well succeed in dangerously increasing royal power. Since Parliament during the 1760s normally supported all of George's ministries by large majorities, the opposition also found it increasingly necessary to argue that Parliament itself and the whole system of government were corrupt. In their quest for place and their attempt to discredit the men in office, the opposition leaders appeared to question the system itself more than they actually did.

Weak within Parliament, Opposition appealed for outside support. They began to experiment with popular agitation by organizing, for their own benefit, the widespread discontent and suspicion of the government that had developed during the years they had been struggling against the king and his ministers in Parliament. The complaints of the excluded politicians would never have been so effective in creating the myth that the king had designs on the constitution if the heavy-handed mismanagement of the Wilkes affair had not increased suspicion of plots against the fundamental liberties of Englishmen. The attack on John Wilkes, occasioned by his scurrilous attacks on the ministry

and royal family in the *North Briton,* both in its initial phases
of the issuance of a general warrant and his prosecutions for
seditious libel and blasphemy in 1763–1764, and in its later
stages of his repeated expulsions from the House in 1769, was a
vendetta against an individual in whose personal favor little
could be said. But the persecution was conducted in a way that
raised basic issues concerning the rights of subjects, electors,
and members of Parliament and the freedom of the press that
Wilkes cleverly exploited to give focus to a developing radicalism in London that called the whole political structure into
question. His radical allies developed a comprehensive reform
program, demanding short (annual or at most triennial) parliaments, comprehensive place bills, binding instructions to members of Parliament from their constituents, the ballot, and a
reform of the franchise. Although the parliamentary politicians
would have nothing to do with such a program, outside agitation
was forcing reform upon them as a political issue.

These differences over the constitutional issues, Wilkes,
reform, and the early stages of the conflict over American policy,
as much as their mutual rivalries for office, turned the factions
in a much enlarged opposition into "parties." All the important
groups—Rockinghams, Chatamites, Bedfords, Grenvilles—
were larger and more unified than the earlier connections out
of office had been. The Rockinghams, particularly, from an
early stage in the conflicts, developed the notion of their connection as an alternative administration, and acted increasingly
in accord with Burke's definition of them in 1770 as "a body of
men united for promoting by their joint endeavours the national
interest upon some particular principle in which they are all
agreed."[8] The other groups also developed distinct identities
and to varying degrees became identified with specific remedies
for some of the contemporary problems.

The formation of these "parties" took the better part of
four years. The two most important and long-lived, the Rockinghams and the smaller group around Pitt, were the first to take
shape, thanks to George III and Bute's anxiety to get rid of the

[8] Edmund Burke, *Works,* Boston, 1865, I, 530.

old ministers and their political friends. When Pitt, the first to go, resigned in October 1761, he went virtually alone; the point on which he chose to resign—the refusal of his cabinet colleagues to agree to his unsupported demand for war with Spain—together with his acceptance of a pension of £3000 a year for himself and a peerage for his wife, temporarily prevented his getting a "party" or indeed much sympathy either in the House or outside. But his eclipse was brief. He rapidly recovered his popularity outside Parliament by his intransigent opposition to the unpopular peace treaties and, although he had no organized parliamentary group behind him and as yet had swayed few votes by his denunciations of the iniquities of Bute's administration and the succeeding one of his own brother-in-law, George Grenville, Pitt soon began to exercise his old magnetism over the independents and some of the younger politicians. Within two years of his resignation he was again looked upon as the principal key to the creation of a stable ministry.

After Pitt's resignation, the duke of Newcastle clung desperately to office for eight more months, despite repeated affronts and constant undermining by Bute and the king. When he finally retired in May 1762, he disclaimed any intention of opposing and urged his friends to stay in office. This they did until more of them were dismissed ignominiously in the autumn for refusing to cooperate with Bute. A few more resigned, but only a fraction of those upon whom the duke had counted. Even then opposition came hard to Newcastle and his older friends. They had come to think of office as their right and expected daily to be recalled as the only men capable of governing. For months the duke and his closest advisers could not decide whether, or how far, to criticize the ministry, even on the crucial question of the peace treaties. This vacillating inner core, however, was gradually pushed into a less compromising position by the junior members of their connection, who were beginning to collect around the young marquis of Rockingham and were meeting regularly at dinners at Wildman's Tavern. By the end of 1763 the Newcastle-Rockingham group had become more of a "party" than any previous group out of office, consistently attacking the ministry and already determined to return to office only as a group, and only in a ministry that they dominated by a monopoly of the key offices.

Because of this insistence on "party" government, to which they adhered with increasing clarity and consistency, they were never able to come to terms with Pitt, even though they realized that union with him was essential to their success. Although Pitt always professed that he intended to base any administration that he formed on the "Great Revolution Principle Families" and to insist on satisfaction for those who had been dismissed in 1762, he would have nothing to do with the Newcastle-Rockinghams as a connection, and above all with the duke himself; he opposed government by "party" as strongly as George himself and regarded the duke with unqualified contempt. For their part, the Newcastle-Rockingham group were unwilling to submit to Pitt's imperious dictation as the price of union, however closely they agreed with him on the proper policy to be followed on most questions before Parliament, and however willing they were to give him and his views a prominent place in any administration they might form. So union—even steady cooperation— proved impossible even after Newcastle retired to the background. This mutual antagonism between Pitt and Rockingham Whigs confounded all attempts at uniting the opposition before Pitt's death in 1778, and personal animus, fully as much as differences in ideas, continued to poison relations among his successors, Lord Shelburne and the younger Pitt, and the Rockingham and Foxite Whigs for the rest of the century. Although this hostility unquestionably weakened the effectiveness of both groups in influencing politics, it also contributed to their growing internal coherence as distinct parties. The Rockinghams were forced to define themselves as a "party" as much *vis-à-vis* the Chathamites as they were in relation to the king and his successive ministers.

The Rockinghams and Chathamites were not the only "parties" to emerge from the political conflicts of the early years of George III's reign. Their original expulsion from the government had by no means deprived the Bute ministry of all aristocratic support. Numerous groups and individuals, most of them part of the original coalition of 1757, remained in office under him and composed the ministry formed on his resignation. Its nucleus was a coalition of George Grenville, who was building up a sizable personal connection in office, and the Bedford group, which had gradually enlarged from a family connection into a "party" by the adhesion of several important peers unrelated to the Russells. When the two groups were dismissed in 1765 after having resisted violently what they thought was the same sort of betrayal by the king and "secret influence" that had driven the "Old Whigs" and Pitt from office, the form of politics for the 1760s had been achieved. There were four distinct groups—Rockinghams, Chathamites, Bedfords, and Grenvilles—plus an amorphous "party" of King's Friends. At least two and usually three of the four distinct groups were always in opposition; nevertheless they were never able to coalesce into a unified party strong enough to force the king's hand.

At times the relations of the four groups with each other resembled those between the prominent individual opponents of Walpole—that is, they were strongly influenced by personal rivalries and jealousies and by clashing ambitions for the same offices beyond the ability of any coalition to accommodate. But these familiar personal elements were now cut across and complicated by serious differences over policy and issues, sometimes the result of honest conviction, sometimes because of the need to defend a position previously taken: Grenvilles and Bedfords felt committed to the taxation and subordination of America and the suppression of Wilkes because these measures had been begun (for excellent reasons, they were convinced) by their joint administration; the Rockinghams had opposed both policies at the time, and had reversed them during their administration, and so were committed to the opposite course. Chatham and his followers agreed in outline with the Rockinghams on both subjects, but differed in details, which removed them still further from an accommodation with the Bedfords and Grenvilles.

The "parties," especially the Rockinghams and the Chathamites, also disagreed on the great constitutional issues concerning the proper relations among king, ministers, Parliament, Parliament's constituents, and the public at large raised by the king's renewed political activity and intensified by the Wilkes affair and American problems. All of them agreed on such platitudes as ending "secret influence" (in which all of them professed to believe) and basing ministries on "Whig principles" and the "great Whig families." But how were these goals to be accomplished? The Rockinghams had the clearest answer, but one which, as they elaborated it, was unacceptable to Pitt, to the other parties, and above all to the king: they would be the undisputed core of the ministry, determining the distribution of places and the selection of measures, independently of their other allies and the king, though hopefully with their acquiescence. These ideas, as they were developed and refined during the next fifteen years, became ever more distinctly innovative, but the essence of the Rockinghamite idea of themselves as a "party" and their aim of "party government" was already apparent by the mid-1760s. They claimed to represent the purest Whig principles and the preponderance of "men of natural weight" in the country; other men and parties, whom they pretended had abandoned their cause for selfish reasons, were welcome to recant and join them, but only in a subordinate role. The mar-

The gouty colossus, William Pitt (Lord Chatham), with one leg in London and the other in New York. London, 1766. *(New York Public Library)*

quis and his friends must dominate any opposition coalition that might be formed, and if they consented to join administration, the existing ministry must be dissolved and totally reconstructed with themselves in all the key positions. The Rockinghams were rather more ambiguous about the king's role; for a long time they seem to have operated in the pious hope that he could be persuaded to see things their way and cooperate wholeheartedly, but as it became clear that he would go to any lengths to escape their tutelage, they eventually determined to force his acquiescence by the crudest political pressure.

These ideas were repugnant to Pitt and only slightly less offensive to the other parties. Pitt clung to older, back-bench "country" notions concerning the relations between the king and the politicians, as did George and the independents. To him "parties," however rhetorically justified, were still nothing more than self-seeking factions that all honest men should root out and destroy in the national interest. The king ought to have an independent and preeminent role as the maker and coordinator of ministries, acting above connections and individual ministers (except, of course, in ministries in which Pitt himself was to be the principal figure, for he always insisted on *"carte blanche"* when asked to form an administration), selecting the men he thought best fitted to serve him and England and insisting that they do so or leave office. But if Pitt was far more backward-looking than the Rockinghams on these matters, he was in advance of them in his views of the proper relations between Parliament and its constituents. Because his political power resulted from his hold over influential opinion outside Parliament itself, he stressed far more than the Rockinghams the responsibility of Parliament to its constituents and beyond them to the public at large; he even professed to favor parliamentary reform to attach Parliament more closely to this public. The Rockinghams, until a small segment of them became "radicalized" around 1780, considered this mere demagoguery. Although they were always ready to appeal to the "people" if they thought it would serve an immediate end, they normally conceived of Parliament, once elected, as essentially independent of its constituents, acting as its own wisdom dictated in accord

with the "true interests" of all Englishmen. Pitt and his followers
were always more ready than the Rockinghams to flirt seriously
with the growing numbers of political radicals.

The Grenville and Bedford parties, although widely
separated from the Rockinghams and Chathamites in their
view of the problem of America, the Wilkes case, and most of
the other specific issues of the 1760s, were closer to the Rockinghams than to Pitt on the constitutional questions. Since the
Grenvilles and the Bedfords, like the Rockinghams, thought
they had been the victims of royal "innovations," they sympa-
thized with the desire to subordinate the king to the politicians,
and had in fact dictated to him in 1765 more peremptorily than
the marquis and his friends had yet presumed to do. But they
were quite unwilling to resume this role merely as appendages
of a Rockinghamite ministry. Since they regarded themselves
as being of equal political weight and as representing equally
pure Whig "principles," attempts at union always foundered as
much on Rockinghamite exclusiveness as on differences on
policy. Furthermore, Grenville, during his ministry, had become convinced that a single, directing ministerial hand was
absolutely essential to administrative stability and efficiency,
so that his conditions for office had come to resemble those of
the Rockinghams; he differed from them primarily in that he
considered himself, not Lord Rockingham, as the man for the
position. He was also willing to consider more extensive struc-
tural changes in the government than they were and he was more
willing to work closely with anyone who professed to share his
political views, regardless of what their recent political past had
been. The Bedfords, although perhaps the most closely knit of
all the parties, were more interested in the emoluments of office
than in power and political consistency and so were open to
coming to terms with any ministry that would meet their price
in places—as Chatham's lieutenants did in 1767—but even then
they maintained their identity within the ministry of which
they had become an important part.

All of these "parties" developed greater internal cohesive-
ness than previous groups out of office had done. Although there
were as yet few permanent political organizations in even the

larger constituencies—such as the Rockingham Club at York—the number of these were growing and they were occasionally taking some interest in wider issues, especially those concerning Wilkes. Political house parties were becoming more frequent—at Wentworth, Chatsworth, Stowe, Woburn, Trenham, at the various race meetings, and (during the parliamentary sessions) at the London houses of the major leaders. Formal "embassies" of the "men of business" (and sometimes even of the leaders themselves) to meetings of each other's groups were increasingly numerous. But the principal party organizations were still the regular dinners for members of the various groups and possible supporters at the London taverns, such as the weekly Rocking-hamite dinners at Wildman's Tavern in the early 1760s and the more occasional ones at the Thatched House at the end of the decade for the temporarily united Grenvilles and Rockingham-ites. Loyalty and union were preached, and strategy was some-times plotted. The amount of advance planning of parliamen-tary maneuvers increased, and the "men of business" and the leaders devoted much time to circularizing their supporters and whipping up votes. Because of a growing sense that each group must act in unison to make an impression in an opposition coali-tion or on the king and ministry, and because of the mounting importance of issues on which taking a stand was unavoidable, the parties were less easily disrupted than the factions of the past had been.

The ministry found it harder to detach individuals from a "party" with offers of places or appeals to patriotism than Walpole or the Pelhams had done, though Chatham acquired a few Rockinghams in 1766, and some of Grenville's original followers soon found their way back to office. Chatham in any case had always exercised a fascination for some of the original Rockinghams, particularly the young duke of Grafton—who became the nominal head of Chatham's administration—and General Conway, who remained as one of his Secretaries of State. But Chatham's ministry, which he attempted to create out of individuals rather than connections (a "tesselated pavement without cement" Burke called it), remained very shaky until his colleagues negotiated a union with the entire Bedford party.

This deal, more reminiscent of the old politics than indicative of the new, contradicted Chatham's own views on the issues of party, of America, and of Wilkes, and was possible only because Chatham, seriously ill, both physically and mentally, had refused to direct his own ministry and allowed his colleagues to drift into measures more popular with the Bedfords than with their own master. When Chatham recovered, he was so enraged by his ministry's actions that he and his closest friends resigned and returned to opposition, where he remained for the rest of his life.

By the early 1770s the opposition parties had been reduced to two, for the Bedfords were now part of North's ministry, and the Grenvilles had disappeared after their leader's death. The Rockinghams and Chathamites, proscribed by the king, and opposed to nearly every act of the now stabilized ministry composed of all their rivals, resigned themselves to a long wait in the wilderness. The Rockinghams had picked up a notable defector from North's ministry, the young Charles James Fox, who rapidly became one of the most influential men in their councils as well as their greatest orator. Together with Burke he further refined and clarified the Rockinghams' evolving notions of "party" and "party government." More strongly than any other politician, he insisted that the duty of men out of office was to oppose every measure of the government. He also went further than his friends had so far been willing to go in his demands that any new administration be formed absolutely independently of the king. Circumstances powerfully aided his arguments.

The American war speeded up the reorientation of English politics along party lines by sharpening the differences between ministry and Opposition, and by making it possible for the two opposition parties to fuse temporarily into a united front capable of imposing more rigorous terms on the king than the politicians had ever done before. Both Rockinghams and Chathamites had consistently opposed the measures that finally drove the Americans to rebellion and had steadily pressed for an accommodation with the colonies, even though the two groups had differed on possible alternative policies. Thus they had completely disassociated themselves from royal and ministerial policy and

The Colossus of the North: or The Striding Boreas.

I'll Stem the Stream

These Are Penitions for Penitions Place have been my Destruction

Lottery Tickets Pension Places

See our Colossus strides with Implicit commands
And Mounted in Corruption's Stream abounds

An Opposition satire on the "corruption" of North's Administration. *(New York Public Library)*

stood instead for a thorough change of men and measures—a true alternative administration. They had also finally succeeded in 1779 in coming to an agreement to work together to bring down the ministry and to form a joint administration to reverse its policy. The origins of the American war and its mismanagement were conclusive evidence to them that the government, through royal interference and divided, incoherent ministries, had become morally and politically bankrupt. The enthusiasm that Englishmen continued to express for the war, until it *really* began to go badly, was taken as evidence of a change in the temper of the governing class, much of which now seemed ready to support every ministerial and royal folly. The Rockinghams and Chathamites, and increasingly other groups outside Parliament, interpreted everything that had gone wrong as the result of the growing influence of the crown—so that a change of ministers and of American policy alone no longer seemed adequate. The influence of the crown must be curbed by law as well. Outside Parliament still more radical measures to reform a "corrupt" system were gaining in popularity. To a few, the success of the American rebellion was a vindication of new and better ideas of government—an invitation to republicanism, even democracy. And in less radical quarters, it seemed that opposition must be right in their declamations that something was fundamentally wrong in the government of England. By 1780 the divisions among Englishmen were more serious than any that had existed since 1714. Not only specific policies, but the whole political system of the preceding years, even the basic institutions of politics themselves, were being called into question. It remained to be seen whether the newer notions of "party" and "party government" being evolved by the opposition could provide an effective answer to these discontents.

CHAPTER FIVE

The Crisis of Eighteenth-Century Politics

All the festering discontent with the political system, long cultivated by the opposition politicians and ignited by military disaster, exploded in a crisis beginning late in 1779 and lasting until 1784. Against a background of popular ferment on an unprecedented scale the parliamentary leaders and the king assaulted one another in terms of clashing views of the constitution. Men outside Parliament, disgusted with the politicians, demanded major changes in the political system, and now, more efficiently organized than before, they forced the politicians to consider reform and to attack the outworks of the long-accepted structure. Even the mob rose and pillaged London for six days, terrorizing the Establishment. The new concept developed by the Rockingham Whigs that the group controlling Parliament should have a free hand in composing the ministry and in

conducting its business triumphed twice—and was twice overturned by vigorous royal action and a resurgence of older views
of the king's proper role in making ministries. Two massive
interventions of public opinion, the first (in 1780) encouraged
by Opposition against the king, ministry, and majority of the
House of Commons, and another in 1784, by the king and ministry against the majority of the House of Commons, affected the
course of politics as the "people" had never before done. The
oligarchy was in fact losing its exclusive monopoly of public
affairs and was being forced to court new groups and to heed
new voices. Contemporaries of every political complexion had
no doubt about the seriousness of the crisis—civil war, perhaps
even social revolution, seemed close.

By the autumn of 1779 Lord North's administration presented a scene of unparalleled debility and internal disarray.
A threatened Franco-Spanish invasion, rebellion in Ireland,
defeats in America, deteriorating relations with Holland and
Russia, and naval reverses in the West Indies provoked only
petty bickering and paralyzed indecision. George III assumed
the initiative in an attempt to galvanize Lord North into action
in order to preserve the ministry and to revitalize the American
war. Acting through his confidants, Charles Jenkinson and John
Robinson, he tried to formulate and enforce some sort of policy
and thereby gave "secret influence" and royal interference more
of a reality than they had ever had before. The effect of his
direct intervention was to destroy any pretense that anybody but
George now created government policy, turning the political
struggle into a direct clash between the opposition and the king.

Long years in opposition had provided the Rockinghams
and Chathamites ample opportunity to develop a coherent and
integrated series of proposals to weaken the crown's influence
in maintaining an inadequate or unpopular ministry in power.
Their program was more realistic than the "stock Opposition
program" of the earlier part of the century, and its appeal was
strengthened by disguising it as a program for economic reform
—that is, for saving money. The opposition proposed to prune
the more obvious sinecures and unnecessary offices in the Royal
Household and elsewhere in order to cut down the number of

places at the government's disposal. The King's Civil List would be regulated to reduce the amount of money available for corruption and influence and to keep the funds for the purposes for which they were intended. Once these measures were carried, Opposition intended to disqualify all holders of government contracts from sitting in the House of Commons in order to eliminate government control over the numerous members who sought or held these contracts. Finally, they proposed to disenfranchise all revenue officers in order to purge the constituencies of the voters most vulnerable to direct government pressure. In the crisis of 1779–1780, this program provided a series of specific remedies for the principal abuse that Opposition had been complaining about since the 1760s—excessive crown influence in the House of Commons.

While the politicians were mounting their campaign for reform against the king and his ministers in Parliament, discontent among the political classes was being organized without their assistance into a vast agitation against the government. The extent and character of the ferment took the opposition leaders in Parliament by surprise. Because the leadership of the movement cleverly added a demand for parliamentary reform to the opposition program of curbing royal influence by economic reform, the politicians could not manipulate the movement to their advantage. In fact most opposition leaders found themselves equally condemned, along with the ministers and their followers, as members of a corrupt oligarchy. Nevertheless, they had to appear to cooperate enthusiastically with the agitation, even while subtly trying to control and limit its objectives, since it offered so strong an endorsement of their thesis that some political reform was essential immediately.

The movement began in the North Riding of Yorkshire in the mind of the Reverend Christopher Wyville, a masterly organizer who knew where he wanted to go and how to get there. In December 1779, in cooperation with other local gentlemen but quite independently of the Rockingham connection, which was so strong in Yorkshire, he arranged a county meeting to petition Parliament for economy in government. By attributing the previous extravagance to undue royal influence, he appeared to offer spontaneous backing to the parliamentary campaign against influence. But this was not all that Wyville had in mind. He proposed to follow up the Yorkshire petition with the creation of a committee of correspondence to continue pressure for granting the petition and to communicate with similar petitioning groups in other counties. Wyville intended that Yorkshire should provide a model for the national organization of the general discontent. He further proposed that the various local committees send delegates to a supercommittee in London to intensify the pressure on Parliament. This central committee of the Associated Counties would act as a national pressure group that would claim to be more representative of national opinion than the Parliament itself.

The movement spread quickly. More than twenty counties and many cities and boroughs petitioned, and in all of them the petitions were generally popular. From the beginning, however, the parliamentary politicians seeking to limit the petitions to the subject of economic reform and undue influence struggled with radicals who wished to add demands for short parliaments and franchise reform. In Yorkshire, Wyville's cunning parliamentary techniques ensured the choice of his candidates for the committee of correspondence and as delegates to the central committee in London, but serious conflicts erupted in other counties. Wyville himself quickly removed to London, and entered into a league with the well-organized urban radicals there. Having assumed direction of the agitation from the center, he proceeded to his next step—a proposal to reform Parliament itself by the addition of 100 new county members and a return to annual elections. Such a program was both too much and too little. By insisting on organic change, he was alienating the country gentlemen who had been his original supporters, as well as the parliamentary politicians; he was also losing the support of the more doctrinaire London radicals because his proposals were moderate. These men were already thinking in decidedly democratic terms about franchise reforms, and not about increasing the number of independent country gentlemen in the House. The leadership of the movement bogged down in speculative disputes within the committees. The addition of parliamentary reform to the Yorkshire program so frightened the independents that the possibility of carrying even the minimum program of economic reform and curbing of influence through Parliament faded.

While the Yorkshire Movement was taking on an increasingly radical flavor, the parliamentary opposition was trying unsuccessfully to put through its own program for reducing the influence of the crown in order to curb the demand for more radical change. In early February Burke presented a detailed plan for economic reform which was well received, but the attempt to enact his proposals was defeated step by step in the course of the next month. The next stage in the parliamentary campaign—Dunning's resolution that "the influence of the Crown had increased, was increasing, and ought to be diminished" was carried against the ministry by 233 to 215, but again remedies to diminish it were all defeated. The reason for these failures was not royal influence or corruption; the government vote remained fairly constant, while that of the opposition varied erratically. The independents were making the decisions —on general propositions they voted with the hard core of the "professional" Opposition politicians, but they abstained from the divisions on particular propositions. Although they opposed influence in general, as independent country gentlemen always did, they could not bring themselves to sanction the invasion of the Civil List and the Royal Household or to consent to serious restrictions on what they believed to be the king's proper role in the selection and coordination of ministries. They thought that the opposition leaders were expounding views of the constitution which were fully as innovating as anything that George had been guilty of.

Charles James Fox particularly alarmed them. While Opposition, by their encouragement of the petitioning movement, seemed to be appealing outside the traditional political framework to the public at large, Fox threatened revolution. Always violent in debate and inclined to demagoguery, Fox had temporarily adopted the most extreme reform measures. The country gentlemen, thinking of themselves as preserving the supposed balance of the constitution, supported Dunning's resolution as a warning to the king to go no further, but at the same time they refused to risk swinging the balance of the constitution too far against him by bringing to power politicians whom they feared might overturn the constitution altogether.

The independents wrecked the reform program. All that was carried was the abolition of the Board of Trade and the vague resolution against influence. George III still had his ministry and his war, while the popular movement behind Opposition was breaking up in factional disputes. Any chance of reform, administrative or parliamentary, disappeared with the Gordon Riots of June 1780 (see page 118), the most destructive that London had ever experienced. The anti-Catholic impulse behind these riots had no connection with the Yorkshire Movement and parliamentary reform, except that both fed on general popular discontents arising out of the unsuccessful American war. But in the background of the Gordon Riots was the Protestant Association, an organization similar in structure to Wyville's Association and employing the same techniques of local and central committees to organize petitions to Parliament. (See page 144.) This agitation aroused emotions that went deeper and affected classes other than the political discontents organized by Wyville—which, after all, glorified the freeholders and the independent country gentlemen with its call for an increase in county members. Even the more radical men in the movement who demanded wider franchise reform were not yet thinking particularly of the lower orders. The urban mass of London and the agricultural workers and tenants of the countryside were still outside the radical interest and program.

The Gordon Riots and the Yorkshire Movement had a profound effect on English political developments as well as on the course of reform. The immediate impact was wholly negative. The terror that the Gordon Riots inspired among the governing class temporarily descredited all appeals to opinion outside Parliament and the political class and all proposals for political or institutional changes of any sort. The opposition politicians were frightened into a temporary cooperation with the government, and there was even talk of a coalition—talk that came to nothing, once the first alarm subsided because

Rockingham and his friends persevered in their demand for economic reform and the end of the war and still insisted on making the ministry their own in accord with their idea of party government. A crisis that began with a flood of petitions against the government, backed by the pressure of organized public opinion on an unprecedented scale, ended with a flood of loyal addresses (the government was also learning the arts of popular appeal) after the "mob" had got out of hand. George III and Lord North seemed to emerge strengthened by the campaign that had been waged against them, whereas the opposition was weakened and discredited.

Nevertheless, reform was far from a dead issue, and the opposition was only in temporary eclipse. Because of accelerating economic and social changes that were altering the basic structure of the country and because of the obvious failure of the old system to cope with new problems, questions of reform would never again be wholly absent from politics. All the groups, even North and his friends, now accepted the need for administrative reorganization, although they continued to differ greatly on the extent and kind of changes to be made and the object in making them. More important still, the issue of parliamentary reform had been introduced into national politics, where it continued to play an important part for the next five years. With economic recovery and a return of political stability the demand for change then subsided, but the issue persisted. It was already causing friction within and between the political groups, although it did not become a major divisive question until the outbreak of the French Revolution. But a few of the Rockinghams, including Fox (although he was never consistent on the question), had been converted to viewing reform as an essential step in reducing royal influence and ministerial corruption, thus introducing the issue into the inner councils of the group. Shelburne and his followers, true to the precepts of their late master, Chatham, proved even more ready to consider some measure of change in the electoral structure.

Nor was reform the only issue: the American problem demanded solution ever more insistently, nothing had yet been done about Ireland, and it was becoming daily more obvious that the East India Company's administration of their new territorial empire needed drastic reorganization. On all these questions the opposition differed radically with the ministry and were as convinced as ever that destruction of the ministry and the creation of a new one, pledged to different policies, was absolutely essential.

Continued military disaster in America soon dissipated North's renewed popularity and gave Opposition its chance to try a "new" system. During the winter of 1782 the government majority rapidly dwindled. In mid-March Sir Thomas Grosvenor, previously a regular supporter of the ministry and informal leader of the independent country gentlemen, delivered the ultimatum that he and his friends could no longer support the government,

> being now convinced that the present Administration cannot continue any longer, they are of opinion that vain and ineffectual struggles tend only to public mischief and confusion, and that they shall think it their duty henceforward to desist from opposing what appears to be clearly the sense of the House of Commons.[1]

The war and the ministry must be ended. George III resisted, but North, who had been trying to resign for three years, finally convinced him that he must give way to the clear will of the House of Commons. North's letter is one of the best expressions of later eighteenth-century political realities:

> The torrent is too strong to be resisted; Your Majesty is well apprized that, in this country, the Prince on the Throne cannot, with prudence, oppose the deliberate resolution of the House of Commons; Your Royal Predecessors (particularly King William the Third and his late Majesty) were obliged to yield to it much against their wish in more instances than one; they consented to changes in their Ministry which they disapproved because they found it necessary to sacrifice their private wishes, and even their opinions to the preservation of public order, and the prevention of those terrible mischiefs, which are the natural consequence of the clashing of two branches of the Sovereign Power in the

---

[1] George III, *Correspondence*, ed. J. Fortescue, London, 1927–1928, V, 394.

State. . . . The Parliament have altered their sentiments, and as their sentiments whether just or erroneous, must ultimately prevail, Your Majesty having perservered, as long as possible, in what you thought right, can lose no honor if you yield at length . . . to the opinion and wishes of the House of Commons.[2]

Three days later the ministry resigned and George was left with no alternative but to give the government to the opposition.

The opposition, although agreed that the king must end the war and accept the economic reform program of 1780, was seriously divided on other issues and rent by deep personal antagonisms. The Rockinghams distrusted, even hated, Lord Shelburne, the new leader of the former Chathamites, who carried on Chatham's and the king's ideal of nonparty government, an administration of all talents. Because Shelburne's views on the structure of administration and his hatred of connections appealed to the king, he favored Shelburne from the first. But the Shelburne group was a much smaller one than the Rockinghams, so that George's insistence that they play an equal role in the ministry caused bitter resentment among the Rockinghams. The new government was clearly a compromise and not a victory for the Rockinghamite view of party government. Although Rockingham, the First Lord of the Treasury, was nominally the head of the ministry, Shelburne and Fox shared effective power. The other offices were equally divided between adherents of the two sides, with the Rockinghams holding a slight majority in the cabinet. The king himself had insisted that the new ministers retain his personal choice, Lord Chancellor Thurlow, from North's administration.

The two parties in the ministry could not agree on how to end the war. Should recognition of American independence precede the detailed peace negotiations in the hope of reconciling the Americans quickly and detaching them from France (as Fox and the Rockinghams wished), or should very generous concessions be made, short of independence, in the hope of preserving an imperial connection, as Shelburne wished? This disagreement was more than a cabinet squabble, for Fox and

[2] *Ibid.*, V, 395.

Shelburne were joint Secretaries of State. Because of a redistribution of the functions of the Secretary's office, Fox was responsible for negotiating the treaty with France, and Shelburne was responsible for negotiating with the American commissioners. Again George took Shelburne's part, because his insistence on maintaining an imperial connection appealed to the king as a means of salvaging something from the wreck of empire. Every cabinet meeting became a battle.

Yet despite acrimonious personal and political quarrels, the cabinet tottered on surprisingly well for three months. The reform legislation was passed: Burke's reforms of the Civil List, Royal Household, and the Pay Office; Crewe's Act disenfranchising the revenue officers; Clerke's Act disqualifying government contractors from seats in the House. A start was also made at fundamental reform through the reorganization of government departments, which would continue after the crisis to transform the character of administration. Irish problems were temporarily shelved by granting Ireland legislative independence and leaving the more difficult problem of coordinating the two equal Parliaments to the future. In settling the peace, the administration accomplished little, and it was over this issue that the breach came, hastened and transformed by the unexpected death of Lord Rockingham.

Rockingham's death provided an excuse to elevate the disputes over American policy and Fox's rivalry with Shelburne into a constitutional principle. The Rockingham ministers insisted that their own duke of Portland succeed Rockingham at the Treasury on the very dubious ground that the king must act only on ministerial recommendation in filling vacancies. When George responded by appointing Shelburne, the majority of the Rockinghams instantly resigned, although they left behind them several former adherents who were unwilling to go this far for the sake of "party" loyalty, when they had no other complaint against the king. The resignation of Fox and his friends won them no support outside their own narrow clique, but it transformed the political situation. There were now three coequal groups in Parliament: Shelburne with his own small following, the remnants of the Rockinghams, and the permanent administration supporters; the Foxites; and Lord North and his friends from the late administration. None of these "parties" commanded a clear majority on their own, and each now professed to abhor the others.

Shelburne carried on for eight months with the king's firm support. The peace treaties were completed, and attempts were made to strengthen the government by a coalition with the Norths or by detaching some of the Foxites from their leader— but all overtures foundered on the uncompromising stance of all groups. More serious still, Shelburne failed to win the confidence of his own colleagues or of the independent members. Because he preferred to work alone, his fellow ministers were given little opportunity to grasp his objectives for reforms. The peace treaties were bound to be unpopular in any case, especially in the absence of any understanding of how Shelburne intended to fit them into a grander scheme of imperial and commercial reorganization.

While Shelburne grew weaker, the most unexpected coalition of all took place when the apparently inveterate enemies, Fox and North, joined forces on February 13, 1783, to bring down the administration. Eleven days later they forced Shelburne to resign by twice defeating him in the House. The principals defended this "unnatural" union on the grounds that the issues that had formerly divided them—the American war and the peace—were now in the past, and there was no reason why they could not cooperate under such changed conditions. There was a measure of truth in this; except on the question of the wisdom of the American war, they were never as far apart as their abuse of each other had implied. But this sort of pleading carried little weight with contemporaries, most of whom were shocked by what seemed the most callous, unprincipled political deal ever made—and made by the very men who professed to be more high-minded and consistent than any of the other politicians. The coalition also destroyed Fox's popularity with the reformers, because he abandoned their program as the price of union with North and his followers, and it completed the ruin of his reputation with the independents, already low because of his violence in debate and his notorious gambling. The union confirmed the worst suspicions of the party now calling itself *the* Whig Party. As one contemporary said, he feared the tyranny of Venice more than that of France.

Regardless of the popular outrage, Fox and North together commanded a majority in the House, and with Shelburne gone, there were no alternative ministers. Nevertheless, George III waited for six weeks, hoping that the new partners would quarrel, while he meditated abdication. But far from quarreling, Fox and North extracted unparalleled concessions from the king. They forced George not only to accept a prearranged cabinet, but also to grant them the right of appointing all subordinate officers. The whole administration was to be composed,

Fox.   Lord North.

The Mask. A satirical attack on the Fox-North Coalition, 1783. *(New York Public Library)*

in Fox's phrase, "independently of the King"—in other words, it was to be a ministry created solely by the leaders of the major-ity in the House of Commons, in which the king was to have no voice whatever. In later generations it could be argued that this majority represented a majority outside the House, but this was not the case in 1783. Party connections and issues played little part in the selection of members, and as far as they had done so in the general election of 1780, a majority of members had been returned as supporters of North and of policies quite the op-posite of those proposed by the Coalition in 1783. The constitu-tional justification for the demands made by the Coalition rested on an assumption of the absolute independence of the House of Commons—from its constituents as well as from the king. On these grounds the politicians defended themselves after George dismissed them while they still had their parliamentary major-ity.

The king, although forced to surrender, was waiting for an opportunity to rid himself of his new masters. His chance came with Fox's India Bill, which reorganized the company and vested control of it in commissioners appointed by Parliament—that is, by the Coalition ministry in actual fact. George engineered its defeat in the House of Lords by authorizing Lord Temple to say that he would regard any peer who voted for it as his enemy. On the following morning he dismissed the ministry and installed the younger Pitt and his friends in office, although they as yet had the support of only a small minority of members. The highly controversial India Bill, however, had already weakened sup-port for the Coalition both in and out of Parliament because it was regarded as an attack on all chartered commercial and mer-cantile interests and as a scheme to establish the Foxites perma-nently in power by vesting all Indian patronage in the hands of their friends. Apart from the hostility engendered by the India Bill, opinion generally was moving in favor of the king and his new ministers, because George had been so obviously coerced by the coalition. The new opposition's majority in the Com-mons—more than 100 when they had been dismissed from office in December 1783—melted away to 1 in March, while the king and the younger Pitt prepared for a general election.

Satire on Fox's election campaign at Westminster, 1784. (*New York Public Library*)

Although the king and Pitt used all the old resources of influence and patronage at the government's disposal and expected to win, they succeeded beyond their wildest dreams. Public opinion among the political classes had expressed itself at the election on an unprecedented scale. The reaction against the Coalition was apparent even in many small boroughs where long-established interests were overturned, and in the open constituencies, where the Foxites and their supporters had been extremely strong in the early 1780s, they suffered a series of humiliating defeats. In Norfolk, Thomas Coke of Holkham, a militant Foxite who had previously dominated the county, abandoned the contest after a canvass, so violent was the feeling against him. In Yorkshire, for two decades safely in Lord Rockingham's interest, the "party's" candidates likewise dared not stand for a poll, so sure where they of losing, and they were defeated in the city of York as well. Fox himself won by so narrow a margin at Westminster that the election was challenged and he had to retreat to a seat for the Orkney and Shetland Islands (controlled by a personal friend) for two years while the election was investigated by a hostile Parliament.

Everywhere in the counties the Foxite union with North had repelled the gentlemen and independent freeholders as an unprincipled bid for power at any price. In the larger boroughs and in the counties too the radicals and reformers—everyone outside Parliament who had been active in the Yorkshire Movement—now supported Pitt, because the new minister was still committed to reform, whereas Fox had abandoned it. The dissenting interest, already strongly identified with reform, shifted sides, as did most of the commercial interests previously associated with the old Opposition. Both groups felt betrayed by Fox and his friends in their bid for power. When the new Parliament met in May 1784, Pitt had an overwhelming majority. The victory was celebrated in a triumphant volume of *Fox's Martyrs*.

For the moment it looked like total victory for the king over the Foxite notions of party government and complete ministerial dominance of administration. Fox and his friends had been largely responsible for their own discomfiture. The violence with which they had expressed their new ideas in parliamentary declamation and private conversation, and the rigor with which they had applied them in coercing the king in 1783, had alienated many men who agreed with their more general proposition that royal influence and ministerial corruption were getting out of hand and needed to be restrained. Indeed the coalition with North suggested that they did not earnestly wish to change the system that North represented. Although no one but the principals could have known that North had prepared for Fox a list entitled "To restore the influence taken away by Burke's Bill, the following places may be given to members of parliament,"[3] the union with him gave the lie to Foxite pretensions "to be men united in principles," and turned their objective into the old bid for power and their specific measures into a means for becoming irremovable in office. Nearly everyone but the Foxites themselves had come to agree with Shelburne's argument in 1782 that if the powers they wished to assume

> of vesting in the cabinet the right of appointing to all places, and filling up all vacancies, should once be established, the King must then resemble the king of the Mahrattas, who had nothing of sovereignty but the name; in that case the monarchical part of the constitution would be absorbed by the aristocracy, and the famed constitution of England would be no more.[4]

Pitt's triumph, however, was a Pyrrhic victory for the king and older views of the constitution and politics. The new minister proved to be nearly as much the master as Fox had demanded to be, although he was a more gentle and subtle one. By contenting himself at first with presiding over an administration composed of a loose coalition of groups and individuals and allowing them a great deal of leeway on specific issues, he soon built up a solid core of loyal supporters in the cabinet and Parliament and assumed an ever-increasing predominance in both until he was able to insist that government supporters accept his views on points he considered crucial.

The king was willing to go along with, even to encourage,

[3] Quoted in I. R. Christie, "Economical Reform and 'The Influence of the Crown,' 1780," *Cambridge Historical Journal,* XII (1956), 146.
[4] William Cobbett, *Parliamentary History of England,* London, 1806–1820, XXIII, 192–193.

his increasing power because the only alternative was the abhorrent Fox. Pitt was also an efficient and reforming minister
and increasingly popular in the country as England rapidly recovered from the disasters of the American war. He became the
symbol of "good government" far removed from the bumbling
inefficiency of the king's "favorites" of the 1760s and 1770s and
from the excesses of the Foxites who seemed to place their own
narrow party interests ahead of the country's. Paradoxically the
man who fulfilled the eighteenth-century ideal of a minister
by obtaining the confidence of the king, Parliament, and the
country at large presided over and encouraged the rapid decay
of the whole eighteenth-century system of politics.

Because of his broad support, Pitt did not need to force
support on controversial questions, and thus he could accept
defeat without feeling compelled to resign—for instance, parliamentary reform, which he had introduced and to which he stood
pledged, lost 248–174, accompanied by what Lord North called
the "horrid sound of silence"[5] in the country. He bowed, probably with relief, to the inevitable verdict of the House and got on
with the business of less spectacular administrative and financial
reform that was gradually, during his twenty years of power, to
destroy the old influence of the crown far more effectively than
the more spectacular reform legislation of 1782 had done, or as
parliamentary reform as it was then conceived could have accomplished. His approach to reform was typical of his whole
approach—to avoid controversy wherever possible with the
king, his own supporters, and even his moderate critics—and
to stick to the business of national recovery from the effects of the
war and the loss of the colonies. And in this approach he seemed
to have judged accurately the temper of the times; men were
tired of violent controversies that had wracked politics in the
early 1780s and threatened to pull the state apart.

While Pitt was consolidating his power the Foxites, shrunk-
en in numbers, and the remaining loyal supporters of North
were successfully regrouping in order to recover something of
their old influence in politics by remaining more firmly attached

[5] *Ibid.*, XXV, 458.

than ever (at least in their rhetoric) to their basic political and constitutional positions. Their resounding defeat in 1784 had resulted in a complete fusion of the two groups. Although Fox and his friends attributed divisive councils to a continuing "conciliabulum" of old followers of North when the party began to break up over the French Revolution, the conduct and structure of the party then, as in the intervening years, does not bear their changes out. Although many of the men who had originally followed North out of office were really Court and Treasury types, these members rapidly made their peace with the Pitt ministry and disappeared from Opposition during 1785 and 1786; the others merged with the larger Foxite group. Most of them, including North himself and Lords Loughborough and Stormont, who became the party's principal speakers in the House of Lords, shared a common outlook on society with the conservative majority of the old Rockinghams and naturally sided with them when the crisis came. But others, such as William Adam, the party's manager and its chief election agent, were closely attached to Fox and remained consistently loyal to him. The opposition was more a unified whole after 1784 than it had ever been before.

To cultivate this unity and to rehabilitate themselves in the minds of the independent members and of opinion outside Parliament, the Foxites developed more of the rudiments of a permanent organization than the group had previously had and gave more attention to steady coordination of their parliamentary campaigns and the preparation for elections. The Whig Club, created in 1784 to organize Fox's supporters in Westminster, was elevated in social status and was expanded into a general club to bring their parliamentary supporters and their principal backers out of doors together regularly during the session. The leading members of the party also encouraged the creation of similar clubs in Westminster and elsewhere to cultivate the inferior classes of voters. A so-called Independent Association in Scotland served similar purposes there. The Whig Club itself was much more than a monthly dinner at which party toasts were enthusiastically drunk by a mutual admiration society. Clerks were hired to circularize members and organize propaganda. The leading members created common election funds, out of which they made contributions to supporters who needed assistance instead of leaving everything to private arrangements as they had done in the past. Electoral activities all over the country, even in constituencies where the leaders had no personal connection, were organized on an ever-expanding scale under the supervision of William Adam and the duke of Portland. A newspaper fund contributed by the magnates was established for subsidies to the friendly press, assistance in the outright purchase of newspapers (the *Morning Chronicle* and the *Morning Post* were both transformed from government to opposition papers in 1788–1789), and the publication of pamphlets. None of this activity was completely new, but it was being undertaken on a previously unprecedented scale.

The impressive facade of unity which the opposition presented in politics during the later 1780s concealed potentially serious internal divisions between a conservative majority centered on the titular heads of the party, the duke of Portland and Earl Fitzwilliam, and a smaller group around Fox, more sympathetic to change. All agreed on the rectitude of the party's conduct and the constitutionality of its every position during the crisis of the early 1780s, but most of the conservative core would go no further. They inclined to lament the degeneracy of the times and dreamed of a golden age in the past when their ancestors had ruled England on true Whig principles without the uninvited interference of the king or the people. They opposed any organic change in the structure of the government and, frightened by the popular tumults of the early 1780s, came to doubt the wisdom of appeals to opinion outside Parliament and the upper levels of the political class. These attitudes were not shared by many of the talented and ambitious younger members of the group, all of them intimate friends of Fox. They wished rather to see Opposition adopt the cause of parliamentary and religious reform, not only because they were convinced that this line would regain the support of reformers and dissenters who had gone over to Pitt, but also because they believed that moderate changes in the constitution would be real improvements. Personal rivalries too were growing up within the party.

The younger members were understandably contemptuous of the capacity of the aristocratic leaders of the connection. Portland and Fitzwilliam were admirable private individuals but possessed only third-rate abilities; the younger activists resented their influence in determining party policy at the expense of Fox and themselves. These young men were also ever more impatient with Burke who, in their opinion, had injured the party by diverting too much of its energy and time to the boring problems of India and by the increasing extravagance of his oratory. Burke, in turn, disliked many of these young recruits, not only because they treated him with scant respect, but also because he disapproved of their ascendancy over Fox and their growing voice in party councils in favor of measures he passionately disapproved of.

These dissensions within the party would have remained as manageable as they had been between 1784 and 1789 had not the French Revolution posed the issues between reformers and conservatives in a new and violent way. The aristocratic, conservative wing of the party shared the general revulsion of the governing class toward events in France while the younger members felt something of the enthusiasm of reformers outside these classes for the dawn of a new and better era: the time had come to make desirable changes in the political and religious structure of the country which would permanently solve the political and constitutional issues of the previous twenty-five years. The old opposition collapsed under these divisions between 1790 and 1792 in the face of the mounting fears of the conservatives that insurrection and foreign invasion threatened more with each passing month. The magnates drifted into a cooperation with the ministry, first on specific measures for repressing radicalism at home and then, after the autumn of 1792, into a general support of the war. A few members went into office during 1793, and in June 1794, the rest of the conservative wing joined the ministry *en bloc*.

Fox and his friends, however, had opposed every one of these moves, ridiculing the fears of their old friends, advocating political and religious reform, and opposing every move by Pitt toward repression at home and war abroad. With the coalition of 1794, they were left a tiny minority in an overwhelmingly

The dagger scene in the House of Commons. *(New York Public Library)*

Pittite Parliament, but a minority sharing the same outlook on every important issue. The opposition now stood for a wholly different approach to political problems from that of the ministry. Subsequent Oppositions, although at times they appeared to revert to the older types of temporary confederations of discontented politicians out of office, never lost this new character of offering a real alternative to the existing ministry; henceforth a major change of men resulted in a complete reorientation of policy. The politicians in Opposition during the eighteenth century, by their rivalries with each other as well as by their common hostility to the ministry of the moment, had turned the mere quest for place and power for themselves into a new convention of the constitution by which a formed Opposition organized as a party became an accepted part of political life, offering unrelenting criticism of every ministerial act.

The Cabinet and the Prime Minister

The most important change in the institutional framework of government in the eighteenth century was the development of the cabinet as the permanent supreme executive body of administration. When its growth was completed, the cabinet consisted of a small group of the principal ministers, normally presided over and dominated by the First Lord of the Treasury, meeting regularly and officially to decide on all important policies to propose to the king and to Parliament. It had assumed not only the administrative functions of the old Privy Council, but also most of the prerogatives of the crown, and by the end of the eighteenth century it had virtually replaced the king as the head of government.

The cabinet took shape as a series of concentric circles of committees within committees of the original Privy Council, each subcommittee more tightly organized than its predecessor. Each new group gradually usurped the functions of its immediate parent body until it turned that body into a rubber stamp for decisions made by the smaller group. The composition of each subcommittee was more and more regularly confined to the holders of the principal offices, with its functions and procedures more carefully defined. Each began, however, as an *ad hoc* solution to a particular situation, so that its exact duties and place in the constitution remained vague. Even in the early nineteenth century, when the cabinet had achieved its final form, one of its members, the third Lord Holland, could still describe it as "legally only a committee of the Privy Council appointed by the King on each distinct occasion," which had "gradually assumed the character and in some measure the reality of a permanent council, through which advice on all matters of great importance is conveyed to the Crown," but which still left the "interior constitution" of the government "vague in the extreme and often irregular and inconvenient."[1]

Nothing resembling the cabinet existed before the revolution, although some of its activities were vaguely foreshadowed by the Privy Council's committee for foreign affairs, which always included the major royal advisers. Because the Privy Council had become unmanageably large under the later Stuarts, with many members no longer in office or even in royal favor, and because secrecy was often desirable, this committee of the principal ministers increasingly worked together outside the main body of the Council, although formally subordinated to it. The king, however, was directly and personally involved in the deliberations of these ministers in a way that he usually would not be after the Revolution, and the subjects discussed were much more narrowly limited to diplomacy and military affairs than they were later. The king was also very apt to make major decisions without any reference whatever to this body or to anyone else in an offical capacity.

[1] Henry Fox, third Baron Holland, *Memoirs of the Whig Party*, London, 1832, II, 84, quoted in E. N. Williams, *The Eighteenth-Century Constitution 1688-1815*, Cambridge, 1960, p. 122.

The change in the king's position after 1688—reflected in the increased responsibility of ministers for all government affairs and the greater regularity with which they met—was a result of special circumstances, not an intentionally devised institutional change. William III was often absent from England, so that a regency was required. This regency invariably took the form of a council whose members were usually the principal officeholders for the time being; the most important of these ministers in turn were given special executive responsibility. In effect, the regency was a kind of select committee of the Privy Council, with an executive subcommittee to handle important matters and prepare business for the larger group. The distinction between these two bodies was quite clear in William's mind. From a sojourn in Holland, he wrote back to England that although he had promised Lord Normanby that he should attend all Cabinet Councils "surely this does not engage either the Queen or myself, to summon him to all the meetings, which we may order, on particular occasions, to be attended solely by the great officers of the crown."[2] These meetings of the "great officers" were always distinguished from the more general meetings of the Council, and William further enhanced their importance by evincing slight interest in the details of English administration and the management of Parliament, provided that his business was done. Because he habitually delegated authority to the holders of certain important offices as such rather than to men as individuals, political opinion was coming to support this practice. Lord Sunderland advised Lord Somers in 1701 that none should be of the Cabinet Council "but who have, in some sort, a right to enter there by their employment."[3]

Further systematization in the conduct of ministerial business and in methods of deciding policy developed after 1701. Business increased greatly because of the war with France, requiring consistent planning of operations and diplomatic negoti-

[2] *Correspondence of the Duke of Shrewsbury*, ed. W. Coxe, London, 1821, p. 33, quoted in E. N. Williams, *The Eighteenth-Century Constitution 1688–1815*, Cambridge, 1960, p. 112.

[3] Philip Yorke, second earl of Hardwicke, *Miscellaneous State Papers*, London, 1773, II, 461.

ations of great complexity. Queen Anne, who was frequently ailing, left more to her ministers in the ordinary course of events than a man would have done, although her influence was never negligible. Her ministers met together in two clearly defined functional groups, one called the Cabinet and the other the Lords of the Committee or simply the Committee. The personnel of the two bodies was essentially the same although their duties differed. The Cabinet met weekly, always in the royal presence. Nine ministers usually attended, with the Lord Chancellor (or Lord Keeper), the Treasurer (or First Lord of the Treasury), the Lord President of the Council, the Lord Privy Seal, the Lord Lieutenant of Ireland, the Commander-in-Chief, and the two or three Secretaries of State members *ex officio*. The presence of other men (Household officers or lesser officers of state) depended entirely on the "quality" and influence of the individual. The main business of this Cabinet was to consider in the Queen's presence correspondence and decisions prepared by the Committee. But it was no rubber stamp, such as the Cabinet Council became in later reigns; Anne's Cabinet discussed the matters before it very carefully, often revising the drafts and altering the recommendations submitted to it. Its decisions were final and could be reversed only by another Cabinet meeting.

The meetings of the Committee were never attended by the queen or her husband; they usually took place at least twice a week with five or six men present. Attendance at this Committee of the Cabinet varied according to the business to be discussed; only the Secretaries of State attended regularly, although all other members of the Cabinet could and did come if they chose. They often met with men who were not members of the Cabinet, but it is clear that such outsiders could come only if they were summoned. The Committee's principal work was the detailed direction of military operations and diplomacy, and in this sense it was an "efficient" body. It could and did discuss everything, but its actions were always subject to the approval of the Cabinet, even in the discharge of some ancient administrative functions which it had inherited from the Privy Council. Despite the fullness of the records of the Cabinet and the Committee, they are virtually silent concerning two of the most important parts of government business at any time—the affairs of the Treasury and the management of Parliament. These matters were discussed in private informal meetings of the two or three principal ministers.

The cabinet procedure of Anne's reign continued for the first three years of George I's, but between 1717 and 1720 it broke down and a new system gradually emerged. The Committee had ceased to exist, and the Cabinet had become a formal organization, much larger than Anne's Cabinet, called the Cabinet Council. The king no longer attended any meetings, not because he did not understand English, but because neither George I nor George II was much interested in anything but the results of their minister's deliberations, and because, if they were present, they had to allow the Prince of Wales, usually connected with the opposition, to come as well. Real power had passed from the large Cabinet Council to a smaller group, known variously as the Inner Cabinet, the Efficient Cabinet, the Counciliabulum, and most descriptively as "the Lords whom the King has usually consulted in all secret affairs"—or briefly, the Lords of Confidence. These men had become the active part of the administration, making all the important decisions. The early development of this group is obscure, but it probably came into being in fact, if not in form, on the collapse of Anne's system.

The government, when the king was in Hanover (as he often was), was officially in the hands of Lords Justices—the whole Cabinet Council constituted as a regency. At such times special arrangements had to be made to ensure that the Lords of Confidence could determine exactly how far the Lords Justices as a whole should be consulted on government business. From the correspondence discussing their procedure in 1739, it is evident that the Inner Cabinet was a long-established body, formally recognized by the king, and that the results of its deliberations were communicated to him in official memoranda. The Lords of Confidence normally included only the two Secretaries of State (Lord Harrington and the duke of Newcastle), the Lord Chancellor (Lord Hardwicke), the Lord President (Lord Wilmington), and the First Lord of the Treasury (Sir Robert

Walpole). Other ministers might attend their meetings, and as many as ten sometimes did; on the other hand, decisions might be made by three or even two of the inner five. They met regularly to confer on all matters of importance, to decide what despatches should be laid before the Lords Justices, and to prepare heads of business for their consideration.

Although the Lords of Confidence submitted more decisions for formal ratification to the Cabinet Council when George II was in England than they placed before the Lords Justices in his absence, their proceedings were wildly unpopular with contemporaries, especially with those in Opposition, who condemned the group as a malevolent invention of Sir Robert Walpole's. As the duke of Argyll complained, "It is not being in privy council, or in cabinet council, one must be in the minister's council to know the true motive of our late proceedings."[4] Nevertheless, the Inner Cabinet survived Walpole to become a part of normal political practice, and control of policy passed more completely into the hands of its members. Finally, during the course of the Seven Years' War, the transfer of executive power from the Cabinet Council into the hands of an inner council of the principal ministers was completed.

By the early 1760s, during Grenville's administration, this inner group had become simply "the Cabinet" to contemporaries, approximating the form of the modern cabinet. The older Cabinet Council continued to exist, but it now met only to hear the king's speech before the opening of the parliamentary session and to confirm or commute capital sentences. The Grenville Cabinet was somewhat larger than the Inner Cabinets of Walpole and the Pelhams, deriving its size from Pitt's War Cabinet of nine created in 1757, when it had been necessary to reconcile conflicting desires between reducing the membership for efficiency (the principle behind the Walpolean Lords of Confidence) and extending it to include in the inner councils of the administration as many as possible of the leaders of the groups composing the coalition ministry. Seven to nine men usually attended

[4] William Cobbett, *Parliamentary History of England,* London, 1806–1820, X, 1137.

Grenville's Cabinets, representing a balance between the heads of the efficient departments and men who were really ministers without portfolio. The group was clearly an "efficient" body, deciding matters of major importance without reference to any other body or person except the king himself. Possibly there was an inner steering group to prepare business for the meetings, but the general pattern of a small group of the major ministers only, meeting regularly and officially, made an inner subgroup less important. And if it existed, it did not develop further to become still another cabinet within the cabinet, as had happened in the past.

No further major changes in the composition or functions of the cabinet took place during the rest of the century, although the Grenvillian organization was polished and refined. Restriction of membership to the holders of certain major offices, already common practice under Walpole and the Pelhams, became so well established that by 1805, when Lord Loughborough (then out of office) claimed the right to attend the cabinet by the king's special permission, Prime Minister Addington rebuked him on the grounds that as Loughborough well knew, cabinet membership was restricted to the principal ministers alone. In the early nineteenth century, the membership again began to increase, but was repeatedly pared back to manageable proportions by successive ministers, finally settling at about a dozen members. Occasional reversions to older practices, such as the inclusion of officers not usually allowed to attend or a direct interference by the king with deliberations and membership, occurred from time to time, but they were always recognized as exceptions to normal procedure and permitted only as temporary expedients to preserve harmony in some specific political situation. Otherwise, the cabinet had assumed its final form of a fully recognized small council of the major office-holders, working together independently of the king and the rest of the administration.

Although the cabinet as the chief executive body of the government was fully accepted by all politicians by the later eighteenth century, the convention of a "prime minister" exercising overriding authority within it was not. As late as 1780 a compiler drawing up an undiscriminating list of royal favorites and principal ministers through the ages still bracketed at least two joint prime ministers for most of the eighteenth century. No one, not even the elder Pitt during the Seven Years' War, exercised authority approaching Walpole's absolute dominance until the younger Pitt achieved a similar position after 1784, and even he was less the complete master of his ministry than Walpole had been or than the late Victorian and twentieth-century prime ministers would be.

During the first half of the century, most men repudiated the idea of a prime minister at all in favor of the old ideal of equal, independent ministers. Samuel Sandys put it admirably in an attack on Walpole in 1741: "According to our constitution, we can have no sole and prime minister: we ought always to have several prime ministers or officers of state: every such officer has his own proper department; and no officer ought to meddle in the affairs belonging to the department of another."[5] Contemporaries tended to confuse prime ministers with the older royal favorites of unsavory memory—a confusion that was not unjustified. It can easily be argued that Walpole was the last royal favorite rather than the first prime minister. He was certainly the last principal minister to make a great fortune out of office—Houghton Hall, the tremendous Palladian palace that replaced the modest ancient manor house of the Walpoles is the still-visible monument. In contrast, the duke of Newcastle spent more than £400,000 of his vast private fortune on government management, and the two Pitts and Lord North repeatedly had to have their debts paid by the king, by Parliament, or by their friends.

Sir Robert's power was in no sense a delegation from Parliament, but came from the favor of George I and II—it was they who allowed him the unfettered use of patronage and influence, which, joined to great personal abilities, enabled him to manage Parliament and to mold and remold the administration to his wishes. Even so, although he packed the administration with supporters and drove out all potential rivals and critics, he was

[5] *Ibid.,* XI, 1232.

always careful to observe the forms of procedure and to appear to act with and through his colleagues, emphatically denying the opposition charges of acting as "sole minister." The royal confidence, however, which had given him authority in the first place, sustained him to the end, and when he finally lost control of the House of Commons, royal favor saved him personally from the vindictiveness of his enemies and placed the new government in the hands of his own followers rather than in the hands of his victorious rivals.

Walpole's successors as principal ministers were each in their individual ways less omnipotent than he had been. The Pelhams were forced for four years to contend with Lord Carteret for the monopoly of royal favor, and even after they had defeated him in the Royal Closet through their control of Parliament, they had to share power with each other. While Henry Pelham intervened everywhere after he became firmly established in office, much as Walpole had done, the jealousy of his brother, the duke of Newcastle, prevented the recreation of the Walpolean monopoly. After Henry Pelham's death in 1754, there was an even more distinct reversion to the older practice of largely independent ministers, whose conduct in their departments was coordinated, not coerced, in the cabinet. Even the elder Pitt, although imperiously demanding that the cabinet accept without discussion his views of military strategy and foreign policy, cared nothing about the details of finance, patronage, and the management of Parliament (the normal domain of the principal minister) and left them all to Newcastle. The revival of ministerial equality was also helped by the balance of the political factions in Parliament during the middle decades of the century, which meant that all ministries were the temporary coalitions of several groups even more than they usually were. There was no one commanding political figure to whose leadership the majority of politicians were willing to submit for long; each insisted on his own independence and his equality with all other members of the government under the king, and on the autonomy of his own group within the ministry and in Parliament.

These divisions among the politicians themselves were as

responsible for the absence of strong ministries during the early part of George III's reign as was the king's determination not to be "enslaved" by the old Whig politicians. George's attitude toward an omnipotent minister in absolute command of the administration is ambiguous. At times he seemed to be searching for just such a man, but another side of his character urged him to adopt that role himself—to be the head of his own administration. He sometimes acted, as his critics accused him of doing, as his own chief minister, but the part was forced upon him rather than intentionally adopted because his choices of principal ministers repeatedly failed him. Grenville quoted George as having told him in 1764 that "it was necessary to lodge the power of government in one man alone,"[6] and George certainly would have done so with Bute, or, after 1765, with Chatham. He also frequently tried to galvanize Lord North to take control of his own ministry. But Bute lost his nerve, Chatham went mad, and North suffered from chronic indecision. All the other politicians—never trusted as these three had been—tried to dictate to him in the old manner.

In any case George, despite his occasional pleas for strength in his chief ministers, always inclined to play off ministers against each other in an attempt to keep the initiative in his own hands, although he usually accepted the advice they gave him individually. His ideal remained to govern above, not through, parties and factions, and when he could not find a minister to do it for him, he tried to do so himself. He succeeded for a time partly because general opinion outside the political factions still held that the king should be free to choose and direct his own ministers within fairly broad limits, and because most men who did accept high office liked being absolute masters of their departments, subordinate only to the king. Beyond these sentiments playing into the king's hands, the factions in Opposition who held different views of the royal position in politics and the organization of the cabinet were too divided among themselves to coalesce under a single leader and force themselves on him.

[6] *Grenville Papers,* ed. W. J. Smith, London, 1852–1853, II, 500.

The result was that for more than twenty years, it appeared that George had vindicated the ideal of nonparty government by reviving the practice of essentially independent ministers. Even the long tenure of Lord North confirmed, not contradicted, this practice, for North was no prime minister in the manner of Walpole, nor even a principal minister as Pitt and Newcastle had been. He was, as he preferred to be, only the first among equals, a role that admirably fitted his own character, usually pleased the king, and delighted most of his major colleagues. "Government by departments was not brought in by me," he told Fox in 1783, "I found it so, and had not the vigor and resolution to put an end to it."[7] Nevertheless, the growing confusion and muddle in administration, the incoherence in policy, and the spectacle of ministers frequently working at cross-purposes were raising serious doubts about the practicability of the old ideas among the major politicians. North himself became convinced that the old system would not do and wrote to the king in 1778: "In critical times, it is necessary that there should be one directing Minister, who should plan the whole of the operations of government, and control all the other departments of administration so far as to make them cooperate zealously and actively with his designs even though contrary to their own."[8] But North was not the man to insist; he was even incapable of being the minister he himself envisioned, so the principal advocacy of a radical view of the proper relations within the cabinet was left to the Rockinghamite opposition.

In their development of the notions of party government expressed through cabinet solidarity under an acknowledged leader, the Rockinghams were far more innovators than George III had been when he helped revive the ideal of independent ministers. They had a leader who provided the chief bond of union in their group and whom they wished to exalt; beyond this they had long insisted that all the chief offices of state should be in the hands of members of *one group*. They believed that

---

[7] Lord John Russell, *Memorials and Correspondence of Charles James Fox,* Philadelphia, 1853, II, 51.

[8] George III, *Correspondence,* ed. J. Fortescue, London, 1927–1928, IV, 215–216.

a party should *make* the cabinet, not merely be offered places in it, and that it should control the whole administration. The Rockinghamites insisted on applying these notions as far as practicable when they attained office in 1782, and they demanded them even more absolutely for the Coalition in 1783.

By the early 1780s, therefore, opinion within and without the government was moving in the direction of the necessity of one principal minister, who could if necessary overrule his colleagues. The king, faced after North's resignation by ministers (other than Shelburne) who were personally distasteful to him, refused to cooperate. Between 1782 and 1784 he did his best to keep cabinets divided, and thus maintain a voice for himself in the government; he even seemed to have won when he secured the defeat of the Fox-North Coalition and sustained the younger Pitt in office without a parliamentary majority. But it was only the appearance of victory; Pitt, in fact, had not inherited his father's views of the royal right to direct the ministry, even though he claimed to share them. But he made it clear that he would accept office on no other terms than effective control of his administration, and the only alternative—Charles James Fox and the Portland Whigs—meant even more exalted claims to ministerial independence and cabinet solidarity.

Other influences too accelerated the movement toward a consolidation of the principal minister's power. George III trusted Pitt implicitly, and was growing less interested in the details of politics than he had been earlier. His first prolonged bout of insanity in 1788–1789 hastened his retreat from business; his correspondence with the ministers became little more than repetitions of their letters to him. The amount of government business was also steadily increasing, especially after war began with France in 1793, so that it was impossible to consult the king in detail as had always been done, at least in form, earlier. Pitt also selected the men who were to fill the major government posts from among his relatives and closest associates, and dropped them if they refused to cooperate; this practice, combined with the definite limitation of cabinet membership to the holders of the chief efficient offices, further consolidated the power of the first minister by turning him, rather than the king, into the maker of the government. By 1803 Pitt was really speaking for all the politicians when he insisted upon

> the absolute necessity there is in the conduct of the affairs of this country, that there should be an avowed and real Minister, possessing the chief weight in the council, and the principal place in the confidence of the King. In that respect there can be no rivalry or division of power. That power must rest in the person generally called the First Minister, and that Minister ought . . . to be the person at the head of the finances. . . .If it should come unfortunately to such a radical difference of opinion, that no spirit of conciliation or concession can reconcile, the sentiments of the Minister must be allowed and understood to prevail, leaving the other members of the administration to act as they may conceive themselves conscientiously called upon to act under such circumstances.[9]

In this sense, the eighteenth century saw a complete change in the attitude toward the idea of a prime minister. Instead of condemning the position as unconstitutional and illegal, the politicians, and opinion generally, now agreed that such a person was absolutely necessary to govern the country. The change parallels the altered attitude toward the cabinet (although neither prime minister nor cabinet was the inevitable result of the other), where men also moved from absolute condemnation to complete acceptance of the institution as a normal part of government. The politicians' behavior still did not always conform to this view of the proper authority of the prime minister in the early nineteenth century, any more than did the actual operation of the cabinet, but divergence in practice was now the exception rather than the rule. Pitt himself resigned in 1802 rather than risk driving the king mad again by insisting on Catholic emancipation, and his weaker successors often failed to exert themselves as forcefully in the cabinet, in the administration, or with the king as he usually did. All of them fell short of his, or Walpole's, normal practice in one way or another, but none ever acted as mere presiding officers as Grafton and North had done.

[9] Earl Stanhope, *Life of . . . William Pitt,* London, 1861–1862, IV, 24.

Chronology

The Restoration, 1660–1688

William III and Mary II, 1689–1702

1689	Jan	The Convention (to Feb. 1690, after Feb. 1689 a Parliament)
	Feb	The Bill of Rights
	May	Toleration Act
	May	War declared against France (to 1697 — War of the Grand Alliance)
1690	March	General election (Parliament continues to Oct. 1695)
		Danby dominant figure in the administration until 1693
1694		Triennial Act (in force until 1716)
		Administration dominated by Whig Junto until 1699
	Dec	Death of Mary
1695		Lapse of the Licencing Act, freeing press from censorship
	Nov	General election (Parliament continues to July 1698)
1697		Treaty of Ryswick, ending the war with France
1698	Aug	General election (Parliament continues to Dec. 1700, dominated by Tories)
1700		Administration reconstructed with Tory dominance under Godolphin
1701	Feb	General election (Parliament continues to Nov. 1701)
	March	Act of Settlement
	Dec	General Election (Parliament continues to July 1702)
1702	March	Death of William III

Anne, 1702–1714

1702	March	Accession of Anne. Marlboroughs achieve power and with Godolphin dominate ministry until 1710
	May	War formally declared against France (War of the Spanish Succession, until 1712)
	July	General election (Parliament continues to April 1705, Tory dominated)
1703	Feb	Dismissal of Rochester Tories

1704	April	Dismissal of Nottingham Tories
	Aug	Battle of Blenheim
	Nov	Defeat of attempt to "tack" the Occasional Conformity Bill to Supply Bill
		Dispute between the Houses in Ashby vs. White
1705	June	General election (Parliament continues to April 1708)
	Nov	Regency Act, neutralizing the place and privy council clauses of Act of Settlement
1706	May	Battle of Ramilles
	Dec	Drift toward Whigs signalized by Sunderland's entry into ministry
1707	May	Act of Union with Scotland comes into effect
1708	Spring	Ministry reconstructed by dismissal of Harley and St. John, and closer union with Junto. Robert Walpole's first major post as Secretary at War
	May	General election (Parliament continues to Sept. 1710)
	Oct	Remaining Junto Whigs receive offices and remaining Tories dismissed
1710	March	Impeachment of Sacheverell; Whigs win but serious Tory riots
	April	Dismissal of Whig ministers begins
	June	Sunderland dismissed
	Aug	Godolphin dismissed; succeeded by Harley (cr. Earl of Oxford and Lord Treasurer May 1711)
	Sept	St. John becomes Secretary of State (cr. Viscount Bolingbroke July 1712)
	Oct	General election (Parliament continues to Aug. 1713, Tory dominated)
1711	Feb	Beginning of Oxford-Bolingbroke feud
	Dec	Occasional Conformity Act against dissenters
	Dec	Marlborough dismissed; goes into exile in Nov. 1712
1712	Jan	Walpole imprisoned in Tower on charges of corruption
	Jan	Peace Conference opens at Utrecht; 12 Tory peers created to ensure carrying it through House of Lords
1713	April	Treaties of Utrecht signed

	Summer	Oxford-Bolingbroke feud becomes serious
	Sept	General election (Parliament continues to Jan. 1715—Tory majority)
1714	Jan	Schism Act against dissenters
	July 27	Oxford dismissed; Bolingbroke has two days of power
	July 30	Anne makes Shrewsbury Lord Treasurer on unanimous advice of Privy Council
	July 31	Death of Anne

George I, 1714–1727

1714	Aug	Proclamation of George I by Privy Council; Regency, dominated by moderate Whigs, announced; Bolingbroke dismissed
	Sept	George I arrives in England
		Ministry dominated by Whigs formed: Halifax First Lord of Treasury
1715	Feb	General election (Parliament continues to March 1722, overwhelmingly Whiggish)
	May	Impeachment of Tory ministers: Bolingbroke flees to Pretender
	Autumn	Unsuccessful Jacobite Rising in Scotland (the '15)
		Bolingbroke breaks with the Pretender
1716	Feb	Remaining Tories in office dismissed
	May	Septennial Act (in effect until 1911)
	Summer	Ministry reconstructed with Walpole as First Lord; Townshend, Stanhope and Sunderland in other principal offices; begin intriguing against each other
		Walpole's Sinking Fund
	Dec	Townshend dismissed
1717	April	Walpole and followers resign from ministry now controlled by Stanhope and Sunderland
		Convocation of the Clergy prorogued indefinitely
1718	Dec	Repeal of Occasional Conformity and Schism Acts
1719	Spring	Unsuccessful Jacobite Rising
	Dec	Defeat of Peerage Bill, intended to limit creation of peers
1720	Winter	Beginning of South Sea Bubble

	April	Walpole and Townshend make peace with ministry and court (return to office in June, with Walpole as Paymaster)
	Sept	South Sea Bubble bursts
1721	Feb	Stanhope dies
	April	Walpole replaces Sunderland at the Treasury (Ministry lasts until 1742)
1722	March	General election (Parliament continues to Aug. 1727)
	April	Sunderland dies, leaving Walpole in undisputed control
		Atterbury Plot (Jacobite)
1723	May	Bolingbroke pardoned and returns to England (restored to his estates in 1725, but never allowed to resume seat in Lords)
1724	April	Carteret dismissed as Secretary of State and sent to Ireland as Lord Lieutenant; Newcastle becomes Secretary of State (until 1754)
1725		Pulteney dismissed
1726		First issue of *The Craftsman,* principal anti-Walpolean journal
1727	June	Death of George I

George II, 1727–1760

1727	June	Walpole succeeds in retaining royal favor through alliance with Queen Caroline
	Sept	General election (Parliament continues to April 1734)
		First Indemnity Act in favor of Non-Conformists
1728		Gay's *Beggar's Opera,* satirizing Walpole
1730	May	Resignation of Townshend; Carteret dismissed; Henry Pelham given first important office as Paymaster
1733	Winter	Excise crisis; Bill dropped in April
	Spring	Chesterfield, Cobham, and other peers dismissed for opposing excise
1734	May	General election (Parliament continues to April 1741)
1736	April	William Pitt dismissed from the Army
1737	May	Licensing Act for the Stage

	June	Quarrel between George II and Frederick, Prince of Wales, comes to head; revival of Leicester House as focus of opposition
	Nov	Death of Queen Caroline
1738	Spring	Opposition opens its campaign for war with Spain
1739	Nov	War declared on Spain (War of Jenkins's Ear)
1741	Feb	Defeat of Pulteney's motion for removal of Walpole
	Spring	War begins with France (War of the Austrian Succession, to 1748)
	June	General election (Parliament continues to June 1747)
	Dec	Walpole's candidate for Chairman of Committee on Elections defeated
1742	Jan	Walpole repeatedly defeated in House of Commons
	Feb	Walpole resigns but ministry remains in being
		Ministry reconstructed with Wilmington at Treasury, Pulteney in cabinet, Carteret as Secretary of State; other offices dominated by Pelhams
		Carteret becomes favorite of George II
1743	Aug	Henry Pelham appointed First Lord of the Treasury
1744	Nov	Carteret forced to resign by Pelhams; leading "Patriots" and some independent Tories from Opposition replace followers of Carteret and Pulteney in ministry
1745	July	Beginning of Jacobite Rising of 1745–1746
1746	Feb	Pelhams and followers resign; king unable to form ministry around Carteret and Pulteney; forced to take back the Pelhams on their own terms; Pitt enters office
	April	Battle of Culloden permanently ends the Jacobite threat
1747	Winter	Prince of Wales again goes into permanent opposition
	July	General election (Parliament continues to April 1754)
1749		Publication of Bolingbroke's *Idea of a Patriot King*
1751	March	Death of Frederick, Prince of Wales
1752		Reform of the calendar
1753		Public furor forces repeal of Jewish Naturalization Act

1754	March	Death of Henry Pelham; Newcastle succeeds to the Treasury
	April	General election (Parliament continues to March 1761)
	Summer	Pitt and Fox decide to attack Newcastle from within ministry
1755	April	Fox reconciled with Newcastle
	Nov	Pitt dismissed; goes into open opposition
1756	Jan	Anglo-Prussian alliance
	Winter	England and France drift into open war (The Seven Years' War to 1762)
	May	Franco-Austrian alliance
	Summer	Disasters in Mediterranean, India, and America
	Oct	Fox resigns; Newcastle and Hardwicke then resign
	Nov ✓	New ministry under Devonshire with Pitt as Secretary of State
1757	April	Pitt dismissed; unsuccessful attempts to set up ministry under Fox
	June	Ministerial coalition between Newcastle, Pitt, and Fox arranged
1759		English forces victorious everywhere
1760	Oct	Death of George II

George III, 1760–1820

1761	March	Bute becomes Secretary of State
	May	General election (Parliament continues to March 1768)
	Oct	Pitt resigns when Cabinet refuses his demand for war with Spain
1762	Jan	War declared on Spain
	May	Newcastle resigns; Bute succeeds as First Lord of Treasury
	Oct	Devonshire dismissed; rest of prominent Newcastle Whigs resign; Fox brought into the cabinet
	Dec	"Massacre of the Pelhamite innocents"
		Preliminaries of Peace of Paris decisively approved by Parliament
1763	April	Bute resigns; ministry reconstructed under George Grenville
	May	Publication of *North Briton* No. 45; ministry proceeds against Wilkes with a general warrant

	Aug–Sept	Abortive ministerial negotiations with Pitt and Newcastle Whigs fail; Bedfords join ministry
	Nov–Dec	*North Briton* voted a seditious libel, not covered by parliamentary privilege
1764	Jan	Wilkes expelled from House of Commons; outlawed when he refuses to return from France for trial
	Feb	Ministry barely defeats motion declaring general warrants illegal
	April	Gen. Conways dismissed from his military commands for voting against government
1765	Feb	Stamp Act passed
	May	King's first mental illness necessitates Regency Act
		King attempts to dismiss Grenville-Bedford ministry but forced to keep them when Pitt refuses office
	July	Grenville-Bedford ministry dismissed; Rockingham ministry formed
	Autumn	News of American resistance to Stamp Act reaches England
1766	March	Stamp Act repealed; Declaratory Act passed
	July	Rockingham and most followers resign; Pitt (now Earl of Chatham) forms ministry
	Nov	Remaining Rockinghams resign
1767	Winter	Important controversy over regulating East India Company
	March	Chatham virtually withdraws from ministry, physically and mentally ill
	Spring	Opposition groups temporarily unify
	May	Townshend duties passed
	July	Abortive ministerial negotiations with Rockingham and Bedford groups
	Sept	Death of Charles Townshend
1768	Jan	Bedfords enter ministry
	Feb	Wilkes returns to England
	March	General election (Parliament continues to Sept. 1744)
		Wilkes elected for Middlesex; numerous riots in London
	Oct	Chatham resigns, goes into opposition. Grafton head of ministry

1769	Winter	Wilkes three times expelled from Commons, declared ineligible, and defeated opponent seated; powerful petitioning movement in his favor during whole year
		Nullum Tempus Act
1770	Feb	Lord North replaces Grafton as First Lord of Treasury (remains until 1782)
		Townshend duties repealed except for tax on tea
	April	Publication of Burke's *Thoughts on the Present Discontents*
1771	Winter	Quarrel between House of Commons and London over printing of debates; last attempt to prevent publication
1772		Dissenters Relief Bill rejected
1773		North's Regulating Act for India
	Dec	Boston Tea Party
1774		Retalitory Acts against Boston
		Quebec Act
		Charles James Fox joins opposition
	Oct	General election (Parliament continues to Sept. 1780)
1775	April	War begins in America with battles of Lexington and Concord
1776	July	American colonies declare independence
1777	Oct	British defeated at Saratoga
1778	Feb	France declares war on Britain
		North's Conciliatory Acts
	May	Death of Chatham; Shelburne becomes leader of his group
		North's unsuccessful attempts to ease restrictions on Irish commerce
1779		Volunteer movement in Ireland threatens rebellion there
1780	Winter–Spring	Yorkshire, or Associated Counties, movement; petitions for economy and reform from all over England
	Feb–March	Burke's proposed economic reforms introduced and defeated
	April	Dunning's motion against influence carried
	June	The Gordon Riots
	Sept	General election (Parliament continues to March 1784)

1781	Oct	Cornwallis surrenders at Yorktown
1782	March	North resigns; formation of second Rockingham ministry, in alliance with Shelburne
	Spring	Beginnings of extensive administrative reforms
	July	Rockingham dies; Shelburne made first minister; Fox and friends resign
	Nov	Peace of Paris with America signed
1783	Jan	Preliminaries of peace with France and Spain signed
	Feb	Fox and North unite and repeatedly defeat ministry; Shelburne resigns
	April	Coalition ministry between Fox and North takes office under Portland
	Nov	Fox's India Bill introduced and carried in Commons
	Dec	Lords reject India Bill; Coalition dismissed; Younger Pitt forms ministry (until 1802)
1784	Winter	Steady shrinking of Coalition majorities
	April	General election (Parliament continues to June 1790)
	Aug	Pitt's India Bill carried
		Beginnings of financial reform and steady extension of administrative reforms
1785	April	Defeat of Pitt's motion for parliamentary reform
1786	June	Beginning of impeachment of Warren Hastings (to 1796)
		Establishment of Pitt's Sinking Fund
		Commercial Treaty with France
1787		First motion for repeal of Test and Corporation Acts
1788	Nov	George III goes insane; regency crisis (until Feb. 1789)
1789	July	Storming of Bastille and beginnings of French Revolution
1790	July	General election (Parliament continues to May 1796)
	Nov	Publication of Burke's *Reflections on the Revolution in France*
1791	March	Publication of Paine's *Rights of Man*
	May	Burke renounces Fox in the House of Commons
	July	Birmingham Riots against French sympathizers and dissenters

1792	Spring	Opposition leaders cooperate with Government in proclamation against seditious libels
		Passage of Fox's Libel Bill, extending the rights of juries
	Autumn	Major Jacobin scare
1793	Feb	Beginning of war with France; conservative part of opposition support war and some members join ministry
1794	May	Treason Trials, which government loses
		Habeas Corpus Act suspended
	July	Fusion of Old Whigs with Pitt's ministry

Bibliographical Note

Because this book has been written with few footnotes and many of the points discussed are still controversial, an extensive discussion of recent literature on eighteenth-century politics is desirable to indicate the author's debts to other scholars as well as to show where the interested student can find other points of view and fuller treatment of most aspects of the subject. The important work that has appeared on economic history has been omitted as bearing only tangentially on the subject, as have studies of foreign affairs and religious history. Most of the books and articles discussed below have been published in the past twenty-five years, since the immense literature, primary and secondary, on eighteenth-century history written before 1950 is fully listed and occasionally appraised in Stanley Pargellis and D. J. Medley, *Bibliography of British History: The Eighteenth Century 1714–1789* (1951). Much of the subsequent work is described in review articles commissioned by the Conference on British Studies by Robert Walcott (1962), William A. Bultmann (1963), and J. Jean Hecht (1966), all collected in Elizabeth C. Furber, ed., *Changing Views on British History: Essays on Historical Writing since 1939* (1966); in the excellent bibliographies in the relevant volumes of *English Historical Documents;* and for the later part of the century, in the bibliography to J. Steven Watson, *The Reign of George III* (1960). There is also a comprehensive list of books and articles on all aspects of constitutional history in E. N. Williams, *The Eighteenth-Century Constitution 1688–1815* (1960); much of the recent literature on politics and administration in the later eighteenth century is discussed in the extensive "Notes on Sources" in John Erhman's *The Younger Pitt* (1969).

The most useful, indeed indispensable, collections of sources for political and constitutional history are E. N. Williams, *The Eighteenth-Century Constitution 1688–1815* (1960); W. C. Costin and J. Steven Watson, *The Law and Working of the Constitution: Documents 1660–1914* (1952); and three volumes of *English Historical Documents:* vol. 8, *1660–1714,* ed. A. Browning (1953); vol. 10, *1714–1783,* ed. D. B. Horn and M. Ransome (1957); and vol. 11, *1783–1832,* ed. A. Aspinall and E. A. Smith (1959). These, of course, present only a minute fragment of the relevant material. The important political correspondences, long available in nineteenth- and earlier twentieth-century editions of varying quality, have been supplemented by further editions in the past three decades. But still greater quantities of manuscripts remain unprinted in most of the public and private collections in England and the United States. The papers of nearly all the major and most of the minor politicians of the century, many of them made available to scholars only since 1945, have survived in great quantities; the government archives are nearly complete. In addition there are the unreliable but nevertheless invaluable sources of pamphlets and newspapers. It is through the exploitations of this mass of primary material that the history of eighteenth-century English politics is being rewritten. Important new source material is included in, for example, the ten volumes of the *Correspondence of Edmund Burke* (general ed., Thomas W. Copeland, 1958–1971), which contain important letters to him as well as his own letters; several of the volumes of the Yale Edition of the *Letters of Horace Walpole,* ed. W. S. Lewis and others, and exhaustively annotated; N. S. Jucker, ed., *The Jenkinson Papers 1760–1766* (1949); J. R. G. Tomlinson, ed., *Additional Grenville Papers* (1962); A. Aspinall, ed., *The Later Correspondence of George III* (1962–1970) and *The Correspondence of George, Prince of Wales 1770–1812* (1963–1971); and the new edition of *The Collected Works of Jeremy Bentham* (1968–   ). The reliability of a major old source, the letters and memoirs of Horace Walpole, is assessed in John Brooke, "Horace Walpole and the Politics of the Early Years of the Reign of George III" in *Horace Walpole, Writer, Politician, and Connoisseur,* ed. W. H. Smith (1967). Most of the other works discussed below also cite extensively from otherwise unpublished material.

Three excellent surveys of constitutional history are available: vol. 10 of Sir William Holdsworth, *A History of English Law* (1938); M. A. Thomson, *A Constitutional History of England, 1642–1801* (1938); and, briefer but comprehensive, chapters V through VII of Sir David

Lindsay Keir, *The Constitutional History of Modern Britain since 1485* (8th ed., 1966). There are a number of serviceable, if rarely outstanding, general surveys of the century or important parts of it: David Ogg, *England in the Reigns of James II and William III* (1955); B. Williams, *The Whig Supremacy 1714–60* (2d ed., 1962); J. Steven Watson, *The Reign of George III 1760–1815* (1960); D. Marshall, *Eighteenth-Century England* (1962); D. Jarrett, *Britain 1688–1815* (1965); Asa Briggs, *The Age of Improvement 1783–1867* (1959); R. J. White, *The Age of George III* (1968); R. W. Harris, *A Short History of Eighteenth-Century England* (1963); J. H. Plumb, *England in the Eighteenth Century* (1950); V. H. H. Green, *The Hanoverians* (1948). K. Feiling's *The Second Tory Party 1714–1832* (1938) is also a general political history rather than a study of a "party," which the author admits did not exist for most of his period. Fifteen important articles on the eighteenth century published in the *English Historical Review* between 1921 and 1962 are collected in *Essays in Eighteenth-Century History*, ed. R. Mitchison (1966). G. Holmes and W. A. Speck, eds, *The Divided Society: Parties and Politics in England 1694–1716* (1967) is a useful collection of documents for the period as is J. F. Naylor, ed., *The British Aristocracy and the Peerage Bill of 1719* (1968) for the years 1717–1719.

Fundamental work remains to be done on the social background of politics, despite all that has been written on eighteenth-century social history. Essential works for understanding the landed classes and the ruling oligarchy are G. E. Mingay, *English Landed Society in the Eighteenth Century* (1963); F. M. L. Thompson, *English Landed Society in the Nineteenth Century* (1963); and four important articles by H. J. Habakkuk: "England," in A. Goodwin, ed., *The European Nobility in the Eighteenth Century* (1953), pp. 1–21; "Marriage Settlements in the Eighteenth Century," *Transactions of the Royal Historical Society*, 4th ser., XXXII (1950), 15–30; "English Landownership 1680–1740," *Economic History Review*, 1st ser., X (1940), 2–17; and "Daniel Finch 2nd Earl of Nottingham: His House and Estate," in J. H. Plumb, ed., *Studies in Social History* (1955), pp. 141–178. D. Marshall, *English People in the Eighteenth Century* (1956), deals primarily with the merchants and "middling sort." R. Robson, *The Attorney in Eighteenth-Century England* (1959), throws light on their activities as election agents and organizers. E. P. Thompson, *The Making of the English Working Class* (1963), emphasizes the growing political and class consciousness of the "lower orders" at the end of the century, and George Rudé's studies, discussed below, have given us our first accurate knowledge of the composition of the "mob."

Political ideas have received a good deal of attention, although there has been no comprehensive study of the period. The most useful survey is still the one in the two volumes of lectures by various authorities, edited by F. J. C. Hearnshaw, *Social and Political Ideas of Some English Thinkers of the Augustan Age* (1928) and *Social and Political Ideas of Some Representative Thinkers of the Revolutionary Era* (1931). The Namierian school, despite their attack on the importance of ideas in determining political conduct, have contributed much information in many of the books and articles discussed below on widely held notions concerning the nature of the constitution, the position of the king, opposition, party, and related subjects. Important new interpretations of Locke's ideas are in C. B. MacPherson, *The Political Theory of Possessive Individualism* (1962), from a Marxian point of view, and in P. Laslett's introduction to his edition of the *Two Treatises* (1960), which demonstrates that they were written at the time of the Exclusion crisis and merely refurbished after the Revolution. Other important recent studies of Locke are J. W. Gough, *John Locke's Political Philosophy: Eight Studies* (1950); M. Cranston, *John Locke, A Biography* (1957); R. H. Cox, *Locke on War and Peace* (1960); M. Seliger, *The Liberal Politics of John Locke* (1968); John Dunn, *The Political Thought of John Locke* (1969); and J. W. Yolton, ed., *John Locke: Problems and Perspectives* (1969). Several articles also emphasize the importance of the Exclusion period in the formation of many characteristic eighteenth-century ideas, among them J. G. A. Pocock, "Machiavelli, Harrington, and English Political Ideologies in the Eighteenth Century," *William and Mary Quarterly,* 3rd ser., XXII (1965), 549–583; O. W. Furley, "The Whig Exclusionists: Pamphlet Literature in the Exclusion Controversy 1679–81," *Cambridge Historical Journal* XIII No. 1 (1957), 19–36; and B. Behrens, "The Whig Theory of the Constitution in the Reign of Charles II," *Cambridge Historical Journal,* VII, No. 1 (1941), 42–71. J. B. Stewart discusses Hume's politics in *The Moral and Political Philosophy of David Hume* (1963).

Radical thought has received particular attention. C. Robbins, *The Eighteenth-Century Commonwealthman* (1959), traces the persistence of a substratum of radical thought beneath the placid surface of politics between the late seventeenth century and the American Revolution, and three books by S. Maccoby discuss later eighteenth-century radical ideas: *The English Radical Tradition* (1952); *English Radicalism 1762–1785* (1955); and *English Radicalism 1786–1832* (1955). A. Cobban, *The Debate on the French Revolution* (2d ed., 1960) is a very useful collection of selections with an excellent introduction. Two studies of William Godwin—D. Fleisher, *William Godwin: A Study in Liberalism*

(1951) and D. H. Monro, *Godwin's Moral Philosophy* (1953)—analyze his political ideas. R. W. Harris, *Political Ideas 1760–1792* (1963) is an illuminating general survey of the thought of the period. The extensive literature on Edmund Burke's thought (listed and discussed in the *Burke Newsletter* [1959–   ]) has been less illuminating than one might have hoped, since much of it is tendentious and is devoted to proving Burke's belief in natural law and the applicability of his every idea to the twentieth century. The best of many books are C. Parkin, *The Moral Basis of Burke's Political Thought* (1956); F. P. Canavan, *The Political Reason of Edmund Burke* (1960); and R. R. Fennessy, *Burke, Paine and the Rights of Man* (1963). The opening chapters of B. N. Schilling, *Conservative England and the Case against Voltaire* (1950) also contain much material on the growing conservatism of English thought during the century.

For the past forty years, all study of eighteenth-century politics has revolved around the work of Sir Lewis Namier, who revolutionized the subject in his *Structure of Politics at the Accession of George III* (1929, 2d ed., revised, 1957) and *England in the Age of the American Revolution* (1930). In both books he concentrated on the Parliaments elected in 1754 and 1761 and on the politics of the first three years of George III's reign, primarily through material in the Newcastle Papers in the British Museum. Nearly all subsequent work on the century has attempted to apply his methods and conclusions to other periods in the century, to follow lines of investigation he suggested, or, occasionally, to challenge some of his conclusions about the character of eighteenth-century politics. In the process, all older interpretations of the century have been fragmented beyond repair; but no satisfactory comprehensive new version, incorporating what is valid in Sir Lewis's interpretation with the modifications that appear essential for all but some twenty years in the middle of the century, has yet appeared. Indeed, many of the pieces necessary for such a study have not yet been assembled, despite all that has been written on the subject.

Sir Lewis Namier's revolution was twofold: methodological and interpretative. His method of investigating the structure of politics—"group biography"—entailed the exhaustive study of all the members of Parliament instead of concentrating on a few leading figures. An analysis of the political structure through the detailed study of all constituencies revealed the patterns of "influence" at the national and local levels and the day-to-day operations of politics. Having cast his net considerably wider than previous historians, he made discoveries that led him to challenge most accepted views of the century, particularly the prevalent Whig interpretation that saw the English constitution under the first three Hanoverians already resembling that of the later nineteenth century. In this version a two-party system existed, producing ministers responsible to Parliament and operating through a fully developed cabinet under the supreme authority of a prime minister; the king had already been reduced to little more than a figurehead, ratifying decisions reached elsewhere. George III attempted to change all this by reasserting royal power, thus violating the constitution by trying to destroy the parties and acting as his own prime minister. Namier rejected every part of this interpretation. Parties in the modern sense did not exist; there were only factions grouped around individuals, and even these included less than a third of the House of Commons; the rest were permanent supporters of any ministry or independents without any party ties. The king, far from being a figurehead, was the real executive with the unquestioned prerogative of choosing his ministers, and he participated actively in every part of his government. George III, instead of violating the constitution, was only acting fully within his legal rights, and those who opposed him, arguing for party government and a reduction of royal influence, were the real innovators. Ideas and principles meant virtually nothing: men acted in politics only in terms of their material interests and private ambitions.

Like all revolutions, Namier's had been foreshadowed in some of the work of the preceding generation. Although the Whig myth in its crudest forms had become enshrined in popular history and textbooks, scholars had long been working toward a view similar to that of Namier's. Although most of them still employed the labels of "Whig" and "Tory" too freely, assumed too precocious a development of the cabinet system and too complete an eclipse of the king (and George III was still an innovator), their accounts contradicted this framework and showed a political reality close to that revealed by Sir Lewis. Among the best of these pre-Namierian works are chapter II in the *Cambridge Modern History,* vol. 6 (1909), by H. W. V. Temperley; D. A. Winstanley's *Personal and Party Government 1760–66* (1910) and *Lord Chatham and the Whig Opposition* (1912); A. S. Turberville, *The House of Lords in the Eighteenth Century* (1927); E. and A. G. Porritt, *The Unreformed House of Commons* (1903); Part I of Elie Halevy's *England in 1815* (1912); and some of the work of Basil Williams. In the perspective of these studies, Namier's version appears more as the authoritative culmination of existing trends than as a total recasting of the history of the century; Sir Lewis and his disciples unfortunately have not been overgenerous in acknowledging the large areas of agreement between them and earlier scholars. Namier further developed and broadened the interpretation begun in his two books in a series of lectures, articles, essays, and reviews. The most important of these (all collected in *Crossroads of Power,* 1962) are his Ford Lectures on "King, Cabinet, and Parliament in the Early Years of George III" (1934) [which survive only in fragmentary form]); "Monarchy and the Party System" (1952); "King George III" (1953); and "Country Gentleman in Parliament 1750–84" (1954).

Namier's students and immediate disciples have applied his techniques, and his ideas, to other periods with varying success. John Brooke, *The Chatham Administration* (1956); I. R. Christie, *The End of North's Ministry* (1958); B. Donoughue, *British Politics and the American Revolution: The Path to War 1773–1775* (1964)—all carry on the detailed narrative and analysis begun in Namier's *England in the Age of the American Revolution.* Betty Kemp, *King and Commons 1660–1832* (1957), surveys the whole relationship from an essentially Namierian point of view. Other scholars have gone farther afield in their "Namierization." Robert Walcott, in *English Politics in the Early Eighteenth Century* (1956), uncritically applied both the method and the conclusions to the politics of the reigns of William and Anne; and Norman Gash has used the method to reach similar conclusions for the mid-nineteenth century, in *Politics in the Age of Peel* (1953). The most important products of the Namier school, however, are five volumes of *The History of Parliament,* three of them edited by Namier himself and John Brooke (*The House of Commons 1754–1790,* 1964) and two by Romney Sedgwick (*The House of Commons 1715–1754,* 1971), the first sections of the comprehensive history of Parliament projected by the History of Parliament Trust, to which Sir Lewis Namier devoted much of the last decade of his life. Although the biographies of all members elected during these years and the studies of each constituency are the materials for history rather than the history itself, they are the *sine qua non* of all future study of the period. The introductory survey by John Brooke to the volumes for 1754–1790 (published separately as an Oxford paperback in 1968) is by far the best work on the Commons, its membership, and the structure of politics for the period. Although generally adhering to Namierian orthodoxy on most points, Brooke considerably modifies the absence of party and downgrading of issues for the 1770s and 1780s. Thus the general tone is post-Namierian in dealing with the politics of the later eighteenth century, and represents a revision of Brooke's earlier view of party put forward in an important essay "Party in the Eighteenth Century" in *Silver Renais-*

sance, ed. Alex Natan (1961), pp. 20–37, and in his *Chatham Administra-tion.* Two other major works, Namierian in general tone but not di-rectly inspired by Sir Lewis and dissenting from his views at various points, are John B. Owen, *The Rise of the Pelhams* (1957), a detailed study of the years 1742–48, and Richard Pares, *King George III and the Politicians* (1953). The latter, the most important single book on later eighteenth-century politics, steers a middle course between the Namierian and neo-Whig versions of the second half of the century. Pares's *Limited Monarchy in Great Britain in the Eighteenth Century* (1957) is an excellent brief but comprehensive essay on the position of the king throughout the century; Owen's *The Pattern of Politics in Eighteenth Century England* (1962) is a useful description of its subject. I. R. Christie, *British History since 1760* (1971) is another similar brief interpretive essay.

    Direct criticism of Namier and the Namierians for their treatment of mid-eighteenth-century politics, the period of their major concentra-tion, is not yet very extensive or thorough. The best statements of the case against Namier's demotion of the role of ideas in history, the over-reliance on the actions of second- and third-rate figures, the concentra-tion on the mechanics of politics, and the excessive legalism of the Namierian treatment of constitutional practices (all of them more pro-nounced in the writings of his disciples than in Sir Lewis's own writing) are found in Herbert Butterfield, *George III and the Historians* (1957). Butterfield defends and restates, with a few modifications, his position in "George III and the Constitution," *History,* n.s. XLIV (1958), 14–33, and "Some Reflections on the Early Years of George III's Reign," *Journal of British Studies* IV, No. 2 (1965), 78–101. His criticism is twofold: first, because the conventions of the constitution were in such a fluid state by the middle of the century (far more so than the Namier-ians would admit), the politicians could legitimately challenge George III's activities—he was trying to ignore the political realities as they had developed in the preceding seventy years and hence was innovating fully as much as his critics. Second, ideas as well as interests inspired many of the leading figures, and they were far more influential in shaping history than were the activities of back-benchers and minor place-hunters. W. R. Fryer has developed an even more thoroughgoing neo-Whig view in three articles: "The Study of British Politics between the Revolution and the Reform Act" and "King George III: His Polit-ical Character and Conduct, 1760–1784," both in *Renaissance and Modern Studies* I (1957), 91–114; VI (1962), 68–101; and "Namier and the King's Position in English Politics 1744–84," *Burke Newsletter* V

(1963) 246–258. He asserts that the Namierians grossly overstate the real influence exercised by George II. The conventions of ministerial government had in fact so hardened by 1760 that George III was acting unconstitutionally in the early years of his reign and again between 1780 and 1784 by his interference in ministerial appointments, his encouragement of divisiveness in his cabinets, and his flouting the will of the majority in the House of Commons. Fryer also sees the king as a far more decisive and enterprising politician than the Namierian portrait of a pathetic, stubborn figure looking for someone on whom to lean. All of Butterfield's and Fryer's criticisms deserve more thorough investigation than they have yet received. The implied answer to them contained in I. R. Christie's negative answer to his question "Was There a 'New Toryism' in the Earlier Part of George III's Reign?" *Journal of British Studies* V, No. 1 (1965), 60–76, by no means settles all the questions raised. Most of the other articles appraising Namier's work that have appeared since his death have been generally laudatory, at least for his treatment of mid-century politics (the most comprehensive are H. R. Winkler, "Sir Lewis Namier," *Journal of Modern History* XXXV (1963), 1–19, and Jacob M. Price, "Party, Purpose and Pattern: Sir Lewis Namier and His Critics," *Journal of British Studies* I, No. 1 (1961), 71–93. The one exception — H. C. Mansfield, Jr., "Sir Lewis Namier Considered," *Journal of British Studies,* II, No. 1 (1962), 28–55 — unfortunately ignores most of the historical evidence on which the answers to the questions he raises must be based in order to concentrate on probable logical fallacies in Sir Lewis's reasoning against despotic designs on the part of the king. The new biography of Namier by his widow (Julia Namier, *Lewis Namier,* 1971) will be essential for understanding the great historian.

The most important and convincing revisions of the Namierian version of eighteenth-century politics have been made for those parts of the century of which Namier did not possess the encyclopedic knowledge which he had of the mid-century: the period between the Revolution and the Hanoverian succession and the last two decades of the century. Walcott's attempt to overturn the views developed in K. Feiling's *A History of the Tory Party 1640–1714* (1924) and G. M. Trevelyan's magnificent *England Under Queen Anne* (1930–1934) by squeezing the politics of the reign of William and Anne into mid-Hanoverian molds has been rejected as inadequate and incomplete. He himself has slightly modified his thesis to admit a greater place to issues, in "The Idea of Party in the Writing of Later Stuart History," *Journal of British Studies* I, No. 2 (1962), 54–61. But his continued denial of real and valid party divisions has been reversed on the basis of much more extensive evidence about the politics of the period, in Geoffrey Holmes, *British Politics in the Age of Anne* (1967); J. H. Plumb, *The Origins of Political Stability in England 1675–1725* (1967); H. Horwitz, *Revolution Politicks* (1968 — a biography of the earl of Nottingham); W. A. Speck, *Tory and Whig: The Struggle in the Constituencies 1701–1715* (1970); and numerous specialized articles on elections, division lists, and specific political incidents. Many of these newer views of the period are presented in essays collected in *Britain after the Glorious Revolution 1689–1714,* ed. Geoffrey Holmes (1969). These establish beyond question the existence of deep-seated and consistent division between Whigs and Tories; although D. Rubini, *Court and Country* (1968), indicates that for much of William's reign the older polarity of Court and Country was temporarily predominant. Rubini's "Politics and the Battle for the Banks 1688–1697," *English Historical Review* LXXXV (1970), 693–714, advances further evidence for his thesis.

At the other end of the century there has been nothing as comprehensive as Holmes and Plumb since Pares's *George III and the Politicians* (1953), but the books and articles bearing on politics emphasize the political transformation taking place. The Namierian methods are generally used, but they are producing a very different picture of politics even in the hands of the Namierians; the extent of the change in interpretation is apparent in some of the papers collected in I. R. Christie, *Myth and Reality in Late-Eighteenth-Century British Politics and Other Papers* (1970). Issues are growing in importance, political organization within and without Parliament is steadily increasing and taking on new forms, political parties are becoming more "modern" and comprehensive, new assumptions about the political structure of the country and the relations between the various parts are gaining ground everywhere. The reform movement and the closely related growth of extraparliamentary agitation and political radicalism have been the subject of a large group of books and articles. George Rudé, *Wilkes and Liberty* (1962), is an important study of the basis of Wilkes's support and the composition of the Wilkite "mobs," as is his "The Gordon Riots: A Study of the Rioters and their Victims," *Transactions of the Royal Historical Society,* 5th ser., VI (1956), 93–114, for that crucial incident in later eighteenth-century politics. Rudé has also written a general study of the London "mob" in the eighteenth century in the *Historical Journal II,* No. 1 (1959), 1–18, and half the chapters of his *The Crowd in History 1730–1848* (1964) also deal with English riots and popular disturbances. The crisis of 1780, both in detail and in some of its wider implications, is studied and somewhat exaggerated in Herbert Butter-field, *George III, Lord North, and the People 1779–1780* (1949) — unfor-tunately published just before much relevant material in the Rocking-ham Papers became available. I. R. Christie, *Wilkes, Wyville and Reform* (1962), links the two stages of the reform movement. E. C. Black, *The Association* (1963) is a careful study of the major extraparliamen-tary political organizations between 1769 and 1793, showing that even the government adopted the techniques pioneered by the reformers to organize opinion in their favor after the outbreak of the French Rev-olution. Further details of the government-sponsored association movement of 1792–1793 can be found in A. Mitchell, "The Association Movement of 1792–3," *Historical Journal* IV, No. 1 (1961), 56–77, and D. E. Ginter, "The Loyalist Association Movement of 1792–93 and British Public Opinion," *Historical Journal* IX (1966), 179–90. Ginter also discusses the remarkable advances made in political organization by the Whig Opposition after 1784 in "The Financing of the Whig Party Or-ganization, 1783–1793," *American Historical Review* LXXI (1965–1966), 421–440, and *Whig Organization in the General Election of 1790: Selec-tions from the Blair Adam Papers* (1967). L. G. Mitchell, *Charles James Fox and the Disintegration of the Whig Party 1782–1794* (1971), is a detailed study of the Opposition in these years. The crisis provoked by the French Revolution in this opposition and the consequent re-alignment of parties along more distinctly ideological lines are the subject of F. O'Gorman, *The Whig Party and the French Revolution* (1967) and Herbert Butterfield, "Charles James Fox and the Whig Opposition in 1792," *Cambridge Historical Journal* IX (1947–1949), 293–330. The later fortunes of the Whig party, now committed to some measure of reform, are discussed in M. Roberts, *The Whig Party 1807–1812* (1939), and A. Mitchell, *The Whigs in Opposition 1815–1830* (1967); both show the continuance of the older personal politics and serious divisions among the groups in opposition as well as the growing co-herence of organization.

   Administrative reform as distinct from political reform has been the subject of a number of important articles. The effectiveness of the Rockinghamite statutory measures to accomplish their goals, indeed the validity of those goals themselves, has been questioned in D. L. Keir, "Economical Reform 1779–1787," *Law Quarterly Review* L (1934), 368–385; I. R. Christie, "Economical Reform and 'The Influence of the Crown' 1780," *Cambridge Historical Journal* XII, No. 2 (1956), 144–154; Betty Kemp, "Crewe's Act, 1782," *English Historical Review* LXVIII (1953), 258–263; E. A. Reitan, "The Civil List in Eighteenth-Century

British Politics: Parliamentary Supremacy versus the Independence of the Crown," *Historical Journal* IX, No. 3 (1966), 318–337. The much greater effectiveness of administrative reform from within in destroying the old bases of royal and ministerial influence in Parliament is discussed comprehensively in A. S. Foord, "The Waning of 'The Influence of the Crown,'" *English Historical Review* LXII (1947), 484–507. F. B. Wickwire discusses the transition of the second-rank administrators from politicians to civil servants in "King's Friends, Civil Servants, or Politicians," *American Historical Review* LXXI (1965–1966), 18–42. Further details of the reforms begun by Shelburne and continued by Pitt are in John Norris, *Shelburne and Reform* (1963) and John Erhman, *The Younger Pitt* (1969). John Cannon, *The Fox-North Coalition: Crisis of the Constitution, 1782–4* (1969) is a comprehensive study. The political and constitutional issues involved are also discussed from nearly every point of view in many of the works already cited. The importance of public opinion in the general election of 1784 is still a subject of controversy. The more recent studies emphasize the role played by opinion: M. D. George, "Fox's Martyrs: The General Election of 1784," *Transactions of the Royal Historical Society* 4th ser., XXI (1939), 133–168; N. C. Phillips, *Yorkshire and English National Politics 1783–1784* (1961). The regency crisis of 1788–1789 is studied in J. W. Derry, *The Regency Crisis and the Whigs 1788–9* (1963). The recent literature on the king's illness is also important for evaluating the king's personality and behavior for other periods as well; two different diagnoses are presented in C. Chenevix Trench, *The Royal Malady* (1964), and articles by Ida Macalpine and Richard Hunter, John Brooke, and Abe Goldberg in *Porphyria—A Royal Malady* (1968) and in Ida Macalpine and Richard Hunter, *George III and the Mad Business* (1969).

The literature on the first two Hanoverians has been far less extensive, and with the exception of John Owen's study of years 1742–1748, and the "Introductory Survey" by Romney Sedgwick in *The Commons 1715–1754* (1971), there have been no thorough analyses of political structure and alignments. Sedgwick's essay is particularly important for its renewed stress on the reality of a persistent Whig-Tory alignment until very late in the period and for its extensive evidence of Jacobite intrigues by most prominent Tories until after 1745. J. H. Plumb's important biography of Sir Robert Walpole (*Sir Robert Walpole: The Making of a Statesman* (1956) and *Sir Robert Walpole: The King's Minister* [1960]) emphasizes his role as the last royal favorite rather than the first prime minister; the first part of the first volume also contains an outstanding portrait of political conditions in the first third of the

century. A. S. Foord's *His Majesty's Opposition 1714–1830* (1964) con-
centrates on the period before 1760. Although he emphasizes the growing coherence and respectability of opposition in these years, the picture that emerges is still one of disparate factions and individuals contending for power. John Wilkes's biography of Henry Pelham, *A Whig
in Power* (1964), argues that Pelham inherited more of Sir Robert's absolute preeminence, although on a parliamentary rather than a royal
basis, than is usually assumed, and hence provides evidence for a real
decline in the king's position in the last two decades of George II's reign.
J. M. Beattie, *The English Court in the Reign of George I* (1967), although primarily an administrative study, emphasizes the central role
of the court in politics during that reign, as does his "The Court of
George I and English Politics 1717–20," *English Historical Review*
LXXXI (1966), 26–37. Romney Sedgwick's introduction to his edition of
Letters from George III to Lord Bute 1756–1766 (1939) lays, definitively,
a number of old myths and emphasizes the tradition of rivalry between
the king and his heir in the politics of the century. John J. Murray,
George I, the Baltic, and the Whig Split of 1717 (1969) is a detailed study
of a crucial incident in early Hanoverian politics.

A number of useful biographies of important political figures
have been published in the past twenty-five years in addition to those
so far mentioned. For the beginning of the period: S. B. Baxter, *William III* (1966) and the less satisfactory N. A. Robb, *William of Orange,
A Personal Portrait* (1962–1966); K. H. D. Haley, *The First Earl of
Shaftesbury* (1968); J. P. Kenyon, *Robert Spencer, Earl of Sunderland
1641–1702* (1958); A. Browning, *Thomas Osborne, Earl of Danby and
Duke of Leeds 1632–1712* (1944–1951); David Green, *Sarah, Duchess
of Marlborough* (1967) and *Queen Anne* (1970); and two biographies
of Robert Harley: Elizabeth Hamilton, *The Backstairs Dragon* (1969)
and Angus McInnes, *Robert Harley* (1970). For the "high" eighteenth
century: J. H. Plumb, *The First Four Georges* (1956); J. C. Long,
George III, The Story of a Complex Man (1960) [disappointing]; John
Carswell, *The Old Cause: Three Biographical Studies in Whiggism*
[Thomas Wharton, George Bubb Doddington, C. J. Fox] (1954); four
studies of Bolingbroke: I. Kramnick, *Bolingbroke and His Circle:
The Politics of Nostalgia in the Age of Walpole* (1968); J. Hart, *Vis-
count Bolingbroke, Tory Humanist* (1965); S. W. Jackman, *Man of
Mercury* (1965); and H. T. Dickinson, *Bolingbroke* (1970); B. Kemp,
Sir Francis Dashwood: An Eighteenth-Century Independent (1967);
G. H. Guttridge, *The Early Career of Lord Rockingham 1730–1765*
(1952); Sir Lewis Namier and John Brooke, *Charles Townshend* (1964);

J. H. Plumb, *Chatham* (1953); O. A. Sherrard, *Lord Chatham* (1952–1958) [unsatisfactory]; C. Chevenix Trench, *Portrait of a Patriot* [Wilkes] (1962); Carl Cone, *Burke and the Nature of Politics: The Age of the American Revolution* (1957); A. Valentine, *Lord North* (1967); A. Valentine, *Lord George Germain* (1962), supplemented by G. S. Brown, *The American Secretary: The Colonial Policy of Lord George Germain* (1963); G. Martelli, *Jemmy Twitcher* [fourth earl of Sandwich] (1962 [an attempted rehabilitation]). For the later part of the century: R. Fulford, *George IV* (2d ed., 1949); Carl Cone, *Burke and the Nature of Politics: The Age of the French Revolution* (1964); J. W. Derry, *William Pitt* (1962); R. Gore-Browne, *Chancellor Thurlow* (1953); L. Reid, *Charles James Fox* (1969); M. P. Mack, *Jeremy Bentham* (1962); P. Ziegler, *Addington* (1965). Alan Valentine has also compiled a biographical dictionary of some 3000 prominent Englishmen in *The British Establishment 1760–1784* (1970); unfortunately it contains many factual errors. Much biographical work needs to be done. No adequate studies of any of the Hanoverian kings yet exist. Such major political figures as the duke of Newcastle, William Pulteney, the earl of Hardwicke (and all the Yorke family), Lord Loughborough, George Grenville, William Windham Grenville, Sir Gilbert Elliot, the duke of Grafton, the earl of Bute, and the marquis of Rockingham—all await full-scale studies, or in some cases, any biography at all. Hardly any studies of the second-rank politicians have been made, except in the excellent but brief articles on those who sat in the House of Commons in the *History of Parliament;* this automatically excludes all the peers. Most of the books on the great aristocratic families, a growing genre, are superficial collections of anecdotes, often of the "see the naughty peer" variety; here, too, much can be done to illuminate the whole subject of political and social history.

Numerous other studies, some of them extremely important, illuminate various interest and political groups and special subjects. P. D. G. Thomas, *The House of Commons in the Eighteenth Century* (1971) is an important study of the practice and procedure of the House; further details of the organization of the Commons are in O. C. Williams, *The Clerical Organization of the House of Commons 1661–1850* (1954) and Philip Laundy, *The Office of Speaker* (1964). A. S. Turberville, *The House of Lords in the Age of Reform 1784–1837* (1958) carries on the study of the Lords begun in his earlier volumes. D. Large, "The Decline of 'The Party of the Crown' and the Rise of Parties in the House of Lords 1783–1837," *English Historical Review* LXXVIII (1963), 669–695 is one of the few other studies of the much neglected subject of the House of Lords. G. H. Jones, *The Main Stream of Jacobitism* (1954) is the best general study of that subject. John Carswell, *The South Sea Bubble* (1960) is the best work on that incident. The relations between English politics and the American Revolution are discussed in most writings on the period 1760–1784. L. H. Gipson's magisterial *The British Empire before the American Revolution* (1936–1969) describes every aspect of imperial political and administrative history, as does V. T. Harlow's *The Founding of the Second British Empire* (1952–1964) for the later period. C. R. Ritcheson, *British Politics and the American Revolution* (1954); G. H. Guttridge, *English Whiggism and the American Revolution* (1942, 2d ed., 1963); I. R. Christie, *Crisis of Empire* (1966) and M. G. Kammen, *A Rope of Sand. The Colonial Agents, British Politics, and the American Revolution* (1968)—all deal directly with the subject. Numerous articles discuss specific incidents, among them A. S. Johnson, "The Passage of the Sugar Act," *William and Mary Quarterly,* 3rd ser., XVI (1959), 507–514, and "British Politics and the Repeal of the Stamp Act," *South Atlantic Quarterly* LXII (1963), 169–188; P. D. G. Thomas, "Charles Townshend and American Taxation in 1767," *English Historical Review* LXXXIII (1968), 33–51; and D. Watson, "The Rockingham Whigs and the Townshend Duties," *English Historical Review* LXXXIV (1969), 561–565. Derek Jarrett, "The Regency Crisis of 1765," *English Historical Review* LXXXV (1970), 282–315, is a careful study of a much misunderstood incident. The study of London in relation to national politics begun by A. J. Henderson's study *London and the National Government 1721–1742* (1945) has been continued by Dame Lucy Sutherland in two important essays: "The City of London in Eighteenth-Century Politics," in R. Pares and A. J. P. Taylor, eds., *Essays Presented to Sir Lewis Namier* (1956), pp. 49–74, and *The City of London and the Opposition to Government 1768–1774* (1959). Her *East India Company in Eighteenth-Century Politics* (1952) discusses the subject thoroughly through the crisis of 1783–1784. The account is continued in C. H. Philips, *The East India Company 1784–1834* (2d ed., 1961). The numerous and frequently clashing economic interest groups of merchants and their impact on politics are surveyed in M. G. Kammen, *Empire and Interest* (1970). L. M. Wiggin, *The Faction of Cousins, a Political Account of the Grenvilles 1733–1763* (1958), examines the weaknesses as well as the strengths of a major family connection. P. Brown, *The Chathamites* (1967), discusses six of the most important members of this connection. B. Bonsall, *Sir James Lowther and Cumberland and Westmoreland Elections 1754–1775* (1960), studies the creation of a small but potent personal connection.

N. C. Hunt, *Two Early Political Associations: The Quakers and the Dissenting Deputies in the Age of Sir Robert Walpole* (1961), details the activities of two early extraparliamentary pressure groups. E. A. Smith, "The Election Agent in English Politics 1734–1832," *English Historical Review* LXXXIV (1969), 12–35, and R. W. Smith, "Political Organization and Canvassing: Yorkshire Elections before the Reform Bill," *American Historical Review* LXXIV (1968–1969), 1538–1560, both describe the growth of political organization on the constituency level. W. R. Ward, *Georgian Oxford* (1958), indicates that the Jacobitism of Oxford University was only "Country" Toryism. Several books have been written on the English press, among them A. Aspinall, *Politics and the Press c. 1780–1850* (1949); and L. Werkmeister, *The London Daily Press, 1772–1792* (1963) and *A Newspaper History of England 1792–1793* (1967). M. D. George, *English Political Caricature: A Study of Opinion and Propaganda* (1959), describes another form of propaganda.

No comprehensive study of British administration in the eighteenth century has yet appeared, although a number of departments and subdivisions, especially in the revenue and those dealing with the colonies, have been the subject of recent monographs: H. Roseveare, *The Treasury: The Evolution of a British Institution* (1969), a general survey; S. B. Baxter, *The Development of the Treasury 1660–1702* (1957); P. G. M. Dickson, *The Financial Revolution in England: A Study in the Development of Public Credit 1688–1756* (1967); J. E. D. Binney, *British Public Finance and Administration 1774–92* (1958); W. R. Ward, *The English Land Tax in the Eighteenth Century* (1953) and articles by him on the administration of the window and assessed taxes, the Office for Taxes, and the revenue commissioners in *English Historical Review* LXVII (1952) 522–542, LXX (1955), 25–54, and the *Bulletin of the Institute of Historical Research* XXV (1952), 204–212; F. B. Wickwire, *British Subministers and Colonial America* (1966); D. M. Clark, *The Rise of the British Treasury* (1960), which deals mostly with its American ramifications; I. K. Steele, *Politics of Colonial Policy: The Board of Trade in Colonial Administration 1696–1720* (1968); R. R. Nelson, *The Home Office 1782–1801* (1969); K. Ellis, *The Post Office in the Eighteenth Century* (1958); Sir John Craig, *The Mint* (1953); J. R. Western, *The English Militia in the Eighteenth Century* (1965); D. B. Horn, *The British Diplomatic Service 1689–1789* (1961).

Much of the already extensive literature on the development of the cabinet has been outmoded by the discoveries of extensive new series of cabinet records for several crucial periods. The best recent summaries are by Trevor Williams, in R. L. Schuyler and H. Ausubel, eds., *The Making of English History* (1952), pp. 378–391 revising his earlier essays on the subject, and in vols. 10 and 11 of *English Historical Documents*. But the following articles are also essential: J. H. Plumb, "The Organization of the Cabinet in the Reign of Queen Anne," *Transactions of the Royal Historical Society*, 5th ser., VII (1957), 137–157; R. Sedgwick, "The Inner Cabinet from 1739 to 1741," *English Historical Review* XXV (1919), 290–302; I. R. Christie, "The Cabinet during the Grenville Administration 1763–1765," *English Historical Review* LXXIII (1958), 86–92; and A. Aspinall, "The Cabinet Council 1783–1835," *Proceedings of the British Academy* XXXVIII (1952), 145–252, which questions the real independence of the cabinet before the death of George IV.

Index

Black Death, 2

Bolingbroke, Henry St John, 1st Vct, 70, 86, 98, 99, 107; administration of, 70, 100, 106, 122, 123; Walpole as described by, 20–21

Boroughs: charters of, 34; government influence in, 81; parliamentary franchises in, 40–42; "pocket," 41, 43, 44; "rotten," 43, 56; typical issues in, 51–52

Brudenell, George (*see* Cardigan, 4th E. of)

Brudenell, James, 73

Buckingham, George Nugent-Temple-Grenville, 2nd E. Temple, 1st M. of, 47, 88, 153

Burke, Edmund, 39, 44, 47, 48, 63, 65, 83, 96, 98, 116, 137, 138, 150, 160; as "man of business," 48, 49; definition of Rockinghams by, 130; economic reforms of, 145, 150, 156

Bute, John Stuart, 3rd E. of, 26–27, 31, 32, 49, 69, 73, 78, 79, 81, 83, 110, 115, 131, 172

Cabinet (*or* Cabinet Council), 36, 84, 88, 149, 150, 156; development of, 19–23, 163–175; "double," fiction of, 25, 27; "Inner," 20, 22, 167, 168; membership in, 22. *See also individual administrations*

Campbell, John (*see* Argyll, 2nd D. of)

Cardigan, George Brudenell, 4th E. of, 79

Caroline, Queen, 26

Carteret, John Carteret, Bn Carteret; 1st E. Granville, 21, 23, 69, 78, 84, 88, 93, 107, 125, 126, 171

Catholicism (*see under* Religion)

Cavendish family, 2, 22

Cavendish-Bentinch, William Henry (*see* Portland, 3rd D. of)

Charles I, 34

Charles II, 3, 34

Chatham, 1st E. of (*see* Pitt, William)

Chathamite party, 48, 59, 72, 76, 83, 130, 132, 133, 136, 138, 140, 142, 149

Chesterfield, Philip Dormer Stanhope, 4th E. of, 28, 89, 93, 98, 107, 125

Chief justices, 22, 31, 32

Church of England (*see under* Religion)

Churchill, John (*see* Marlborough, 1st D. of)

Civil List, 33, 142, 145, 150

Clive, Robert Clive, 1st Bn, 62

Cobham, 2nd Vct (*see* Temple, Richard)

Coke, Thomas, 155

Commons, House of (pages as listed and *passim*): composition of, 28–36; conduct of business in, 92–96; corporate powers of, 33; East Indian interest in, 63; financial supremacy of, 18, 23, 33; Fox, Henry, as manager of, 22, 85; lawyers in, 31–32; management of, 38–39, 70–92; "men of business" in, 48–49, 137; merchants and financiers in, 32, 56–58; military personnel in, 32; principal ministers in, 93–94; purchase of seats in, 7, 62, 81; relation of, to executive, 33, 68, 84, 148–149; Speaker of, 96; West Indian interest in, 60–61. *See*